Solution States

A Course in Solving Problems in Business

With The Power of NLP

By

Sid Jacobson

Published by The Anglo American Book Company,
Bancyfelin, Carmarthen, Wales

First Published in the UK by

The Anglo American Book Company Ltd
Crown Buildings
Bancyfelin
Carmarthen
Wales

British Library of Cataloguing in Publication Data
A Catalogue record for this book is available from the British Library.

ISBN 1899836039

Printed and bound in Wales

Dedication

This book is dedicated to the late
Todd Epstein.
It would not exist without his help,
teaching and friendship of many years.

List of Figures

SOLUTION STATES:
A Course in Solving Problems In Business
With The Power of NLP
by Sid Jacobson

Table of Contents

Acknowledgments

The author would like to acknowledge and thank the following people and sources for their help and guidance as well as permission to use their material, without which this work would have been far less intelligible.

This book began, partly, as a collaboration with Robert Dilts in whose debt I'll remain. The work, of course, is mine so any limitations or flaws are mine alone. I also appreciate Bobby's continued collaboration, support and friendship which enriches me as well as it has so many others. He is responsible for many of the most useful ideas in this book including the Neuro-Logical Levels, The Seven C's and much of the work on identity.

The contributions of the late Todd Epstein cannot be adequately acknowledged here. His work in developing some of the basic principles of NLP, especially in the area of sub-modalities and the conceptualization of the problem space and how to expand it, are central to this book. Our many discussions of these ideas, and of applying NLP to all areas of living, will always be important parts of my personal growth and history.

Thanks also to Dixie Hickman, Ph.D. and her husband Glenn Oehms for developing the SPACE model for project development. This model also appears, and was originally developed for, Dixie's and my book The POWER Process: a model for writing. I have adapted it here.

A special thanks goes to my wife and long-time companion Cindi Jacobson for putting up with me for all these years. The same to my parents, brothers, in-laws, nieces, nephews and other extended family, for the same reason.

A special acknowledgment goes to my many students and corporate clients over the years who have helped me develop, fine-tune and verify the usefulness of all the ideas in this book. Like most works of this type it is the outgrowth of workshops I've conducted for many years, in a variety of countries and settings, with thousands of clients.

No book on NLP is complete without acknowledgment and thanks to Richard Bandler and John Grinder, co-developers of the ever-expanding technology of Neuro-Linguistic Programming. Their genius, collective and individual, has seldom been matched in the field of human behavior and systems thinking.

Introduction

For The Reader, Evolving

Does *Solution States* fit?

I recently had the opportunity to hear a brilliant anthropologist named Jennifer James warning a large group of training and development specialists against practising "management by bestseller". Probably no need to worry with this book. Also, there is no need to worry that this book will run counter to whichever paradigm you are currently operating in (or pretending to). Whether you are aiming for "Excellence", TQM, CQI, a learning organization, a total process re-engineering (probably to get one of the others), or the next new management development framework, what you have in your hands will help and support you.

All business and management paradigms have one inescapable thing in common: reliance on a particular piece of equipment. Your brain. Business will never be something you can do totally by the numbers, no matter who says so (aren't you tired of "The three sure fire ways to close every sale ..." or "Four quick steps to solve any problem ..." or "If you only do this one thing, everything in your life will change completely, overnight, as if by magic so you can have wealth beyond your dreams and a Winnebago for your wife and kids..."). Unfortunately, we will have to be able to *think* to do a good job, at least in the foreseeable future. When that changes, I'll let you know.

Cracking the code

I remember growing up loving spy movies. My favorites always had some guy with a microfilm plan of the latest weapon, reduced to a dot the size of the head of a pin. Looking under the microscope it looked like hieroglyphics from some lost civilization. The guys in the lab always promised to "crack the code" and catch the villains. They usually did. In NLP we've cracked a lot of codes. They have to do with how people think and learn. The nice thing about

1

cracking a code is not only what you find the *first time*, but that you can do it over and over, *anytime* you need to. That is what this book is about. Not a quick fix for your problems. Not a list that says "turn to page seventeen for the answer if your problem involves three idiots, a computer and a mule". It's about cracking the code to your own thought processes so that you can use those processes the way they were designed.

There are a lot of questions you'll need to answer for yourself along the way. Remember this is much more than solving a current problem, though that is certainly one goal. Once you crack the code to your own thought processes, what you find will be there for you to use for a lifetime, in solving problems, thinking creatively and more.

Also, I don't intend this to be the final word on this subject. It is one phase in the evolution of this system of thought, about thinking. We have enough knowledge now to compile some of it in a useful form that makes sense in a book (there is lots more that I think is best learned in a class, a seminar or under the guidance of a consultant). It may seem complicated to you if this is your first exposure to this field of knowledge. Just remember, a few years from now, it will seem overly simplistic, even childish, the way most things you learn do as you evolve. That's the goal.

Though all of us in the field of NLP know these things work, we would never ask you to take that on faith. When we learn something, we constantly test our findings and results–including on ourselves. If something works for us, we pass it on and see how many others it will work for. In the process we usually discover some people or things it won't work for, as well, then we refine it. I've been using the processes you're about to discover for years. This book is your invitation to join me in this continual process of discovery, refinement and evolution.

What *Solution States* is For

What are problems?

There are some major problems with problems. Sounds strange, doesn't it? But listen to that statement *literally*. The major problem with problems is that they force us into thinking from a deficit position, rather than a resourceful one. There is a saying that goes, "If you *think* you have a problem, then you *have* one." Those of us who have had certain kinds of training don't generally think about problems in that sense. We are oriented, because of our training, to think primarily about outcomes & goals. In other words, pick a direction, or a specific thing we want, then figure out how to get there, or it. Instead of problems, we would rather talk about achieving excellence, or potential, or growth. That's fine. But the *reality* is that most people don't think in those terms; and many who say they do, *act* as if they don't.

In business, and most of life, people still work from a problem orientation. That is certainly how America generally operates. In fact, there may be a built-in problem in expecting people to simply adopt a growth, excellence or quality orientation in place of their already existing problem orientation. It has to do with, of all things, states of consciousness, a major part of this book. When someone is experiencing difficulty, or a problem of some sort, he or she is not in a state of growth or excellence, or even thinking about those things. More likely is a state of confusion, pain, anger, or some other unpleasant emotion. That is part of the goal of this book: to help you get out of these self-defeating, *problem perpetuating states*, and into more useful ones.

A second problem is also built into this sense we have of our problems. Most of us are trained from an early age to respond to problems, barriers, and blocks with an avoidance reaction. We've learned to move *away from* problems or pain. This is very different from moving *toward* goals or pleasure. It requires looking and listening for different things in our environment and in the world as a whole. In this sense, it is dependent on different "perceptual filters".

This concept of perceptual filters is a way of talking about our individual ways of seeing, hearing, feeling, interpreting and understanding the world around us. We build filters based on our experiences, perceived successes and failures (and traumas). Most of us have forgotten where, and when, we learned to use the particular filters we do. This makes us slaves to them, until we re-discover our own processing styles and preferences.

In addition, these filters come in a variety of flavors we'll be discussing throughout this book. One major set of filters is called Meta-programs (programs that run *other* programs, i.e. our behavior). Meta-programs are used to describe a basic orientation people take, almost an attitude, in certain contexts or situations. These Meta-programs determine what we look and listen for–even what kind of information we're able to process. In a state of avoidance, or pain for that matter, your attention is, out of necessity, focused on the discomfort or whatever is causing it, often to the *exclusion* of anything else ("When you're up to your ass in alligators, it's difficult to remember that the original goal was to drain the swamp"). We all, at one time or another, have treated *potential solutions* as annoyances or distractions, because we were so focused on our bad feelings.

Making the transition from an orientation of avoiding pain, to one of seeking pleasure, is not really what this book is about. It is, however, about the transition from problem orientation to solution orientation. Rather than fight against the natural tendencies that we have all learned so well, we can acknowledge those tendencies and use them to our best advantage. I've built a model, based on tried and true NLP technology, that does this. That's what we'll be focusing on and learning. My intention is to guide you, step by step, through the change in orientation, while simultaneously helping you solve problems. Learning this will help you make that important transition automatically, from now on. In that sense, what you have here will be *generative*. That means it will work for you more and more in the future, like a snowball rolling down a hill, gathering size, substance, and momentum. What you have thought of as problems, up to now, may very soon seem like something else entirely.

Neuro-Linguistic Programming

This technology is from a field of study called Neuro-Linguistic Programming (NLP). NLP was developed in the early 1970's by Richard Bandler, Ph.D., an information scientist, and John Grinder, Ph.D., a linguist. It grew out of their research into the structure of communication, and how people influence one another, at the University of California at Santa Cruz. The actual technology, or methodology, of NLP is human modeling: building models of how people perform or accomplish things (any things–see Appendix IV: *A Look At NLP's Underside* for more on this). NLP is also based on an attitude that anything that someone can do can be duplicated by others. The combination of this attitude and methodology has created lots of applications and techniques in a variety of fields.

Those of us working in the field of NLP have been applying this technology to a variety of endeavors for many years. Years ago, we started off thinking "remedially", in other words how to solve problems, mostly of a personal nature. In fact, psychotherapy was the first widespread area of application in NLP. There were a number of reasons for this orientation, but that isn't really what NLP is about. Rather, it's a technology geared toward helping people to communicate better, make needed changes, and achieve their goals–by cracking codes. During the code-cracking process, though, an *orientation* toward problems usually has to be gotten over. Also, some problems get solved.

In problem solving, because there are so many different workable approaches, I've used a combination of the different kinds of modeling tools NLP has to offer. Also included here are some standard procedures that are useful in all problem solving. Because of the nature of this beast, it's possible to apply lots of ideas and techniques that would not normally be associated with solving problems at all. One of these is the area of whole brain functioning. Most people, by now, are aware of the differences between the two sides of the brain and the way they function. Many tasks favor the kinds of things one half of the brain does over the other. So we say those tasks are "right brain" or "left brain" intensive (really an oversimplified way of talking about it). It implies that, somehow, people are to "choose" which parts of the brain they apply to which activities. Though these choices are certainly unconscious, we do seem to actually make them. Overall, in solving problems the whole brain needs to be used effectively, like in most other activities. The procedures you'll go through in this book will get you to use your whole brain in the way it was designed to be used.

This means, ultimately, a combination of logic, intuition, and feelings. Some people believe that solving problems is simply a matter of applying logical brain power ("left brain") to the difficulty, until it is reasoned away. Certainly there are many occasions when this is the case. Other people tend to favor following their gut feelings, or intuition ("right brain"), over their logical judgments. This can also be an effective way. No matter what a person's bias is, eventually he or she will run into a problem in which the "favorite" half of the brain will fail to come up with a workable solution. One obvious way to overcome this inevitable block is to include both logic and intuition in the process. A good solution to a problem should look, sound, and feel right–all at the same time–logically *and* intuitively. That means applying the best technology available to help us use our brains effectively.

Working With The Solution States Process

Solution States relies on NLP skills and techniques. It's designed to insure that:

1. Problems can be properly framed and understood.
2. Workable solutions can be developed.
3. These solutions can be properly fitted to the problem at hand.
4. They can be successfully implemented.
5. The results can be tested against some measurable standards.
6. The learning gained can be used in the future.

Within the model are skills for clearly defining a problem, choosing the result you want, getting into a state in which you can creatively develop a solution, "pre-testing" the solution, carrying it out, and measuring your results. All of this will take into account the type of person you are, and whether or not the solution violates any of your personal values or causes any other kinds of problems. It also takes into account any of the other people who may be involved in solving the problem (or, more importantly, may actually be the problem) so that everyone involved "wins". (I assume, here, that win-win situations are the ones we should all work toward, whenever we are dealing with other people of good will. There may, however, indeed be situations in which this is not possible.) This model also includes ways of refining solutions, and helping you to avoid future similar problems, or more readily solve them if they come up. The effectiveness of the model is limited only by your ability to be in touch with your own internal resources, and your careful attention to each step in the process. I'll help you with both.

Creativity & decision making

A note on creativity is in order here. People often say to me, "Oh, *creativity*–no problem–I just don't have any." Wrong. Everyone has some ability to be creative. We have all successfully solved problems and come up with unique ideas. Many people just don't give themselves enough credit for it. As you go through the instructions, it will become clear to you, if it isn't already, that you have all the tools you really need to solve the problems you experience. Generally you just need a different framework, or point of view, in understanding the real nature of each problem and perhaps a better state to creatively come up with solutions.

As much as possible, without making the book too heavy to lift, I'll try to give you brief examples of solving work problems of different forms. These problem types are: Personal (individual) problems; Interpersonal/Communication problems; Training problems; Systemic problems; and Environmental/Situational problems. Within these, there are fifteen sub-categories.

The reasons for this breakdown are several. For one, I want to be able to provide enough specific examples from different areas so that you can find something that applies closely to you and a current problem you are experiencing. In doing that, you may find that more of the examples apply than you originally thought (or were willing to admit). Also, it seems that it is often better to learn about problems of different types than your own, to be able to solve yours. That's because sometimes you can see some things more clearly without any emotional involvement, and then apply them to your own situation later. Much of this will involve making adequate decisions about what applies to you, and what doesn't. In fact, it's probably obvious that decision making in general is a major part of all problem solving. So you'll get specific decision making strategies as a part of the whole package. You've already made one good decision: picking up this book. You'll make more by continuing to read and working carefully toward your solutions.

The NeuroLink

Much of what you are going to learn is aimed at getting you into the best possible state for creating solutions and solving problems. Simply doing the exercises will demonstrate and teach you the procedures. There is, however, advanced technology that can aid you further in both learning and continuing to generate these powerful states for yourself.

If you have a personal computer, you can use the NeuroLink. This is a system that *connects you to your computer* in such a way that the computer can measure certain basic functions in your body like heart rate and temperature. It can then give you (bio)feedback and help you adjust your state of mind so that you get into the state you need. Though we concentrate on problem solving for this book, of course it can be used in a number of other situations to enhance your performance. Appendix III will tell you how to get the equipment, both hardware and software, that you'll need. Remember, though, this is an additional advantage you can use for yourself–*everything in these pages will work* with or without *the NeuroLink*.

Overview of the book

This book is divided into two main sections. Part I will help you in Defining Your Problem SPACE, the first step in figuring out how to solve any problem. You'll learn ways of viewing your problem or problems that may help you make an immediate change. You'll learn about the SPACE your particular problem occupies and how to work within it, or expand it, to get to a solution. The SPACE Model is an acronym that stands for **S**elf, **P**urpose, **A**udience, **C**ode and **E**xperience. You'll also learn how to make sure that your goals are well designed and measurable. There's a chapter for each of these pieces.

Part II will take you through the NLP technology of eliciting Solution States. This will help you to understand how your mind and body function together to create your state of consciousness, and how you can control it, so that it doesn't control you. You'll learn how to use your past successes and your best internal resources to solve current problems and prevent future ones. You'll also learn ways of understanding how systems function, including organizations and businesses, so that the solutions you develop make sense within these larger frameworks. This includes refining your measurements for effectiveness and motivating yourself to move through the solutions you develop smoothly and gracefully.

Finally, there is an Appendix section that outlines and summarizes a number of useful procedures for you. This will be especially useful in the future to refresh your memory and help you program yourself to automatically use what you have learned here. One section will show you how to use the

NeuroLink technology along with what you have learned in Part II. This will include programming the exercises into the computer so that you can repeat them quickly and relatively effortlessly with the help of the bio-feedback provided by the NeuroLink.

The best use of this book

You'll go through a great many new ways of thinking in the first half of this book. You'll learn about a number of processes for identifying the root of any problem. You'll also be asked to do a great deal of thinking, and deciding about who you are, what you want, and what you know. In the second half of the book you'll go through some fascinating procedures for changing and controlling your thinking, feelings and state of mind.

To get the most value out of this book, it is designed as a training course you can take at your own pace. There is no reward for finishing quickly. There is, however, a tremendous prize for those who go through all of the processes *thoroughly*. They will change your work, and your life, in some wonderful and lasting ways. So take the time, and use your energy, to answer the questions and to do the experiments diligently.

I have designed the questions and experiments for you to apply to a particular problem or situation in your work (though they will be just as effective if you choose a problem or difficulty from your personal life). Pick a problem or situation you truly want to make a change in and keep it in mind while you answer the questions and do the experiments. You may even want to choose several, since very rarely will any difficulty last all the way through the questions in the first half of the book, much less the experiments in the second half.

I suggest you have a notebook, or at least some paper, handy so that you can make lists, jot down ideas, answer questions and so on. There are forms in the second half of the book you will want to have a number of photocopies of, for later use. You'll be instructed on how to use these when you get to them.

A Special Note To The Practitioner of NLP

This is a very unusual book, as NLP books go. It is neither a standard form of text nor a set of workshop transcripts. There are no real "case studies" (though there are examples and metaphors). It is designed as a self-study course, and as such it is extremely sequential. It will be difficult to "dip in" randomly anywhere in the book, and still get the same benefit from what you find as if you go from start to finish. It is also not intended to be swallowed whole, all at once. Those of us in NLP who are careful to be thorough in our work, know the importance of understanding and appreciating the structure of whatever we are unpacking. This book is my attempt to structure an approach to that unpacking, so that you clearly see, hear and feel the structure of whatever problems you choose to explore.

When you began to learn NLP, it may have seemed overwhelming, both in the acquisition of skills and in the sheer volume of information. But when you began to chunk these down, practice techniques and play with alternative ways of thinking, you undoubtedly found it a worthwhile and fascinating journey. One with no end. My hope is that this book will widen, and even smooth, the road for you.

What you'll see in Part I is much of the conceptual framework underlying NLP itself, and our beliefs about thinking, communication and change. It is organized in a way that includes questions meant to help instill these beliefs as well as clarifying your identity, framing or reframing your approach to problems, and organizing your choice of interventions. You may realize things as you go through these questions that send you immediately into your bag of NLP goodies to solve problems. That's great. My intention in this book is to help the NLP'er to do that well, and hopefully, more logically and directly. My intention with those not familiar with the technology is to introduce it in a way that will give them enough to solve any problem, and also to go much deeper into the technology than I have here.

Part II is an introduction to states (4-tuples), sub-modalities, anchoring and the uses of these ideas and tools in problem solving in business. As you will recognize, this concentrates the solutions to those that can be gotten through changing stuck states to something more useful–it can be thought of as a state-based model for problem solving, though the way it is presented involves more levels of analysis than that. The actual "intervention" is a modified Change History with some additional features from the Logical Level Alignment exercise and some perceptual position work. If you are familiar with these techniques, you probably also know that if you do this well, and thoroughly, you can solve just about any problem; even ones that exist on the belief and identity level, as well as those that are behavior and capability centered. That's not to suggest that this is the best, fastest or most elegant way to solve any problem. With the other skills you have you will undoubtedly combine what you find here with lots of other ideas and techniques to find the most elegant ways.

In addition, I intend this as an aid to any consulting you may be engaged in with others (you'll notice I didn't specify *which* others, business, personal or ...). I have been doing, modifying and expanding this model for over ten years with many clients and businesses and organizations. It has been tested over and over.

Keep in mind also that we can all benefit from lots of questions asked in new ways and in different sequences. Remember that NLP began with a set of questions about how experts process information. These were based on a set of presuppositions that were operationalized as well as stated, then a model of asking even better questions, based on specific patterns in people's language. I did not include the Meta-Model, specifically, in this book for a variety of reasons, but you can certainly remember to have it active in your thinking as you go through the questions that I did include.

This book then, for the Practitioner of NLP, is an invitation and a challenge. An invitation to use your skills, within a framework that makes sense. And a challenge to use all of your other knowledge and skills to make your experience of going through this book even richer than what, I believe, is on the actual pages. Enjoy!

PART I

Part I

Defining Your Problem SPACE

Overview

Defining the Problem SPACE is the most important first step in solving any problem. It is something we all do naturally, but seldom systematically. That is why we often find, later, that our ways of looking at our problems actually were the cause of them to begin with.

In Part I, I will introduce you to the SPACE Model that has proven effective in several fields in addition to problem solving. SPACE stands for **S**elf, **P**urpose, **A**udience, **C**ode, and **E**xperience. In Defining the SPACE of your problem you will need to identify your role in the problem, who you are in essence, your **S**elf. Next you need to decide what it is that you really want to accomplish, your outcome, goal, or **P**urpose. Next is who will be watching you, benefiting from, or suffering from what you do.   The other people involved are your **A**udience. Next is the **C**ode you have developed in defining this problem up to this point, and how you might want to change it. In other words, how have you been thinking, sensibly or not, about the problem, and communicating it to others. Finally we have all of your **E**xperience to draw on. This is the sum of information you have, and can obtain, on what to do to make a change in the problem situation.

At the end of these five chapters, you will have totally examined your problem SPACE. By the time you are ready to really step back and take a good look at the SPACE you have defined for this problem, you may realize that it is totally different than you originally thought. It may not even be a problem anymore.

Figure 1

The Problem SPACE

SELF	PURPOSE	AUDIENCE	CODE	EXPERIENCE
Motivation Means Opportunity	Well-Formed Outcomes	Who is Involved, Affected, Observing	Deletion Distortion Generalization	Problem Types: Personal Interpersonal/ Communication Training Systemic Environmental/ Situational
Identity: Presuppositions	Personal & Business Values	Relationship and Task	Thought Viruses & The Seven C's	
Identity: Role	Alignment of Outcomes and Values	Sorting Styles	Neuro-Logical Levels	

CHAPTER 1

Self

The first thing that is important in solving any problem, in business or anywhere else, is in knowing who you are as a person, what we call identity, and your role in the problem. Without a clear idea of your relative position in any situation, you can't be sure that any plan you implement will actually fit. There is no wrong way to take a look at your role, other than not to do it at all. So, the question becomes, "Where do I start?" Well, there are specific things to think about, especially in terms of your beliefs and values, that I know will help you begin this process in an organized fashion.

First, do you believe you can make a difference? Obviously, if you don't think you have any control over coming to a solution, you won't be very effective. In fact, if you don't believe you can do anything about it, why bother? Of course you may believe that you can do what needs to be done, only to be undercut by others who may be involved (maliciously or not). That kind of thinking won't help much either. In fact any "negative" thinking will probably get in your way sooner or later. Best to get it out of the way first.

Basic Presuppositions

One great place to start in exploring anything is to look at its underlying assumptions, or *presuppositions*. In NLP, we have a useful way of thinking about people, their problems, communication, needs and values. In fact everything we do in NLP stems from these basic beliefs. It is not necessary that you agree with all of them; they are simply the ones, we believe, that allow us to be effective. Perhaps looking them over will get you thinking about your own basic assumptions, and how they might be at the root of this problem, or others you run into. Spend a little time on the questions and, if you can, take notes. They'll help.

Presupposition #1: The map *is not* the territory.

This is a very old way of saying that our beliefs and ideas about how people, life, and the world work aren't necessarily accurate. They are just a guide, or map, of how things work. In this world, people don't act on things because of the way those things actually are. Rather, they act on their own personal *maps* of how they are. It may be that you have been following some old rules or guides in your work (an out-of-date map) that are actually getting in your way, rather than helping you. Maybe it's time for a new map.

Questions:

1. Do you run your business affairs (or your life) from some rigid set of rules? Where did they come from? Is it possible that, though they were effective back then, they aren't as valid now?
2. When was the last time you realized something you believed was *incorrect*? How did you handle it, and change your thinking?
3. Can you remember a time when you *expected* something to occur, and something very *different* happened instead? How did you adjust to this difference between expectations and actuality?
4. Have you ever found yourself disagreeing, or even arguing, with a co-worker or business acquaintance about some theoretical issue you had little or no *direct* experience about? Were you able to "catch" yourself and admit that your ideas were just that, only ideas? Did you interrupt the argument and agree that the two (or more) of you simply had different viewpoints, each of which could enrich you?
5   Do you find changing your beliefs and expectations easy? How have you managed these changes when you've done them really well?

Presupposition #2: All behavior has some "positive" intention. People make the best choices they perceive are available to them.

No matter how weird you think other people's (or your own) behavior is, there is some good reason behind everything that they (or you) do. Sometimes you have to do a great deal of questioning and thinking to get it to make sense, but with patience and perseverance it will. Maybe you get stuck at certain times in your work and don't yet know why. Or perhaps you believe that people you work with are evil, dangerous, stupid, or just don't deserve to have you around. This kind of thinking can make your task very difficult, or even painful. If you assume that you have a good reason for being stuck, and that the other person has a good reason for being however they are being, then it can change your thinking enough to get you going in a better direction. You'll learn more ways later.

Questions:

1. When you've been confronted with situations in which people have acted strangely, how have you managed to "step back" from the situation and make sense of it?
2. Have you ever asked this question: "How is it possible that someone could think or behave this way?" Or: "Under what circumstances (or in what context or specific situation) would this kind of thinking or behavior make perfect sense?"
3. If you were to imagine that you could see the world with the innocence and naiveté of a child, how would this (or any) situation look different? How would you change to adjust?
4. Was there ever a time when you thought someone was doing something to hurt you, but later realized they were really intending to help?

Presupposition #3: The meaning of any communication is the response it elicits, regardless of the communicator's intent.

It is really easy to blame others for misinterpreting what we want them to do. Good communicators, in other words good business people, take responsibility for getting others to understand them. People respond to what they think they hear, see, or understand. Assume that people are responding appropriately, then figure out *how* you got them to do it or *what* they must be responding to. It will make you think and communicate differently. You'll also understand people much better.

Questions:

1. Can you think of a time when you gave someone careful instructions and they did something totally different from what you meant? Has this ever happened, and later, with clear hindsight, you understood how that person could have done what they did? Did this ever happen in a way that convinced you that you were ambiguous in your communication?
2. Can you remember an occasion in which you responded with anger to someone, only later to realize that you had misunderstood them? Did you promise that person, or yourself, to be more careful to understand from now on?
3. Have you ever made the conscious decision to be the best communicator you can possibly be?
4. What would your work (life) be like if you made the assumption that people responded appropriately to you all the time? Would it make you figure out how you get them to do the things they do, regardless of your actual intent? Would it make you think differently, and understand the people around you much better?

Presupposition #4: The mind/body relationship is cybernetic, a change in one part of the system will affect other parts.

Most people realize that our thinking affects us physically, even to the point of making us sick (or well). By the same token, if we are not healthy, or even comfortable, we won't think very well. Think about how difficult it is to make reasonable, rational, intelligent decisions when we are upset or angry. If we learn to control our physical and mental processes effectively, there is very little we can't do. And let's not forget our immediate surroundings, our environment. We should live and work in one that is supportive of who we are and what we need, both individually and collectively.

Questions:

1. How long has it been since you stopped to "take stock" of how you run your life, and your health?

2. What changes would you need to make in your thinking, the way you treat your physical needs, or your environment to give yourself every opportunity to live life to its fullest and healthiest?

3. When has there been a time when you realized the importance of using your mind to control your physical well-being? To exercise? Quit smoking? Lose weight? Become motivated, energetic?

4. How do you insure that you get a good diet, enough exercise, plenty of rest, and lots of healthy stimulation to keep vital?

Presupposition #5: There are no mistakes, only outcomes. There are no failures, only feedback.

Every thing we do, successful or not, can be learned from. If we take results as feedback, they can teach us a lot about how to behave and live. People who kick themselves for their mistakes usually don't take the time to carefully analyze the causes and effects; they're too busy kicking. They don't learn all they can. Those who don't learn from their own history are condemned to repeat it.

Questions:

1. When was the last time you found yourself consoling a friend or loved one who had screwed something up? Did you notice how you did this with an attitude of support, without harsh judgment, realizing that, even though the outcome may have been lousy, the intentions of this person were worthwhile?

2. Have you ever done the same thing for yourself?

3. What were your biggest "life lessons"? The ones that have shaped you in the most positive ways?

4. Have you ever heard, or said to someone else: "Someday you'll look back on all this and laugh?" As NLP co-developer Richard Bandler would say, "Why wait?"

Presupposition #6: Everyone has all of the internal resources they really need (which doesn't mean they couldn't use a little help finding them).

People are resilient. They are smart. They are capable (this means you *and* the people you work with). When they don't seem to be any of these things it is because they are not in touch with their natural internal resources and strengths. Probably it's a cliché we get tired of hearing, but the best help is the kind that gets people to help themselves; to use their own talents and abilities.

Questions:

1. We've all had the experience of doing something foolish, or seeming to forget how to do something, even when we really know it well. Later, when the situation has passed, we realize that we knew exactly what to do, but were just too flustered at the time to gather our wits about us. After any of those times have you ever stopped to "pre-program" yourself (in whatever way you do this)? - in other words, to make sure that you would handle the situation in a planned out, rational and capable way, if it ever arose again?

2. Have you ever forgotten something, perhaps someone's name, or another important piece of information, only to "spontaneously" remember it at a later time? Have you ever wondered what it would be like to be so in tune with your unconscious mind that you would be able to remember these things when you need them? Have you done any experiments that would help you in this area before?

3. How much time do you spend actually planning how you would handle difficult situations? Do you vividly imagine these things occurring, and feel the feelings you would have if you smoothly, effectively and gracefully moved through these difficulties?

4. Do you often imagine that each day you'll have more and more of your abilities and resources available to you, automatically?

Presupposition #7: All the information you need can be obtained through clear and open sensory channels (eyes, ears and feelings).

We all know that we sometimes look around wildly, and needlessly, for that which is right in front of us. Whether this is our car keys, the pencil we just put down, the right person for the job, or a new idea–if we pay attention we can find it. If we don't, we can't.

Questions:
1. Do you realize that people tell you and show you everything you need to know to deal with them effectively?
2. Have you ever had an experience in which *time* itself seemed to *slow* down to the point that you were able to see and hear much more than you seem able to normally?
3. When was the last time you stopped to just look and listen, when you needed to make a change? Did you notice new things when you did this? Things that made a real difference for you?
4. What would your life be like if you easily noticed all of the subtle cues and messages others around you gave out in their everyday communication?

Presupposition #8: An effective person (communicator, in business and life) needs three characteristics:

1. Flexibility of behavior to get results.
2. The sensory acuity to notice the results.
3. The good judgement to know whether the results are worth getting.

Many problems are created by doing the same things, over and over, whether they work or not. The old saying, "if at first you don't succeed, try try again" needs to be amended to, perhaps: "... try try again, in a new and different way." From the field of cybernetics (the study of systems; both electronic ones and human thinking ones), there is a law: "The law of requisite variety: The part of any system with the most options in its behavior will be the part that is in control of the system."
            Flexibility = options = control. Simple.
Also, especially when you're trying something new, you have to pay close attention to see the results. This goes for people and things. Finally, you need to keep in mind that just because you *can* get something done, that doesn't make it a *good idea*. We should consider our results in relationship

to all the other things that they can affect. In business, we can "get on a roll," and at the same time lose sight of our overall goals and the reasons we do what we do.

Questions:
1. When have you realized that, though you were trying your best, you were doing something that, fundamentally, wasn't going to work? How did you adjust your actions?
2. Have you ever had the opportunity to be "tested" by life in a way that demanded extreme flexibility on your part? Did it make you better able to handle difficulties creatively?
3. If you had to "let go" of one overly rigid thinking pattern, belief, habit or other behavior, *today*, which one would it be? How would this change affect you?
4. When was the last time you stopped something that seemed to be working just fine, simply to question your own judgment and motives about whether it was really worthwhile?

Presupposition #8 Corollary 1: Resistance is a sign that:
Either
Rapport has not been effectively established or maintained;
Or
Objections have not been properly considered and addressed.

We often hear people in business complain that others don't, or won't, go along with their ideas. These are the two reasons. You have to establish rapport, a working relationship of understanding and trust, usually just to get people to pay attention, much less to agree. Also, you have to be willing to listen to, respect, and respond to the concerns or fears of those you're involved with. The best, most persuasive, communication in the world won't overcome poor rapport or legitimate objections.

Questions:
1. Have you ever had a great idea, but been so eager to tell others about it that you "bowled them over" in your excitement? How did you repair the loss of rapport, and try again, in a more respectful way?

2. Has anyone ever done something that adversely affected their relationship with you? How did you make the decision to patch things up, even if it wasn't really your responsibility? Did you decide that the relationship was more important than something petty, like the need to be "right" or "in control" in the situation?

3. When presenting ideas or plans to someone, how much time do you give them to voice all of their concerns and objections? Do you then treat that person with the respect they deserve, and take the time to answer their questions?

4. If you automatically remembered to consider the relationship aspects of all your interactions with other people, in how many ways would your work life, and the work lives of others, improve?

Presupposition #8 Corollary 2: There is no such thing as a dangerous or unethical process or technique, only dangerous and unethical users (people). It is up to us to know the difference and act accordingly.

Influencing others, running a business, making decisions–these things are neither good nor bad. Again we must decide that what we're doing has a purpose that is worthwhile. If our intentions include a good and worthwhile outcome for everyone involved, it would be silly, and could even be harmful, *not* to use our abilities to influence others.

Questions:
1. When has there been a time that you have used some advantage, or influence, over someone, that was *truly* in that person's best interest (*not rationalized*)?

2. Have you ever been afraid of, or concerned by, some new, very powerful, information or technology? Have you vowed to use it only for the best of reasons, and in the best way you know how? Could you now?

3. Have you ever stopped to think of all the marvelous, but potentially destructive, tools we have around us, even in our daily lives? Do you operate all of them with an attitude of respect and appreciation? Isn't this what it means to be truly safely conscious?

4. If you were to insure that you could use all of your knowledge to make your work life the most enjoyable and worthwhile it could be, for everyone involved, what changes might you need to make?

Presupposition #9:   If it is possible in the world, it is possible for anyone. It is only a question of how.

If you believe you are very limited in your abilities you will act as if those limitations are real. They're not. Act as if you can do anything others can do, and it will motivate you to find out how they do it. Then you can too.

Questions:

1. When was the last time you really impressed yourself?
2. How would you go about learning something, now, that you have always wanted to, but avoided or made excuses about?
3. Is there someone you know who needs to be reminded that we are *all* capable of just about anything worth achieving?   Is there anything stopping you from reminding that person NOW?
4. If you actually behaved as if you could achieve anything you wanted to, how would you be different? When?

I have a lot more questions for you. For now, how do you feel about this list of basic beliefs? Do you agree that they are worthwhile having? How do you think your beliefs affect any problem you may be having now, or problems in general?

Roles & Identity

You see, the main thing about these basic beliefs, or any others, is that they help us orient ourselves to who we truly are, as people. This is different from who we are in relationship to others–or at least it should be. A person who has a firm grasp of his or her own identity, who truly "knows" himself or herself, seldom gets caught in the trap of indecisiveness. That doesn't mean that they can't have some doubt about certain roles they have chosen to take on. But it does mean that if some confusion about that role occurs, there is a basic sense of self they can fall back on to make decisions. This isn't esoteric or complicated. The main point is that *who* you are, and *what* you do, are two different things. And the choice about what you do needs to rest firmly on who you are, not the other way around. If not, you will experience a constant juggling of roles and behavior that will make your decisions, and your life, quite difficult. This is what happens when a person constantly tries to change to suit any job, or role, he or she takes on. It works a lot better to take on those *that support who you are* as a person, and make you an even better one, than to try to adjust to a role that fundamentally does not fit. Adaptation is a healthy and powerful force, up to a point. Here are some more important questions along these lines, ones you can ask yourself:

1. Am I sure of who I am as a person, and how this affects me in my work?
2. What role am I playing in this problem, or in taking on the responsibility of solving this problem? Is it my usual "normal" role in my job, or outside of my normal role?
3. Have I, perhaps, taken on more than one role? If so, are these various roles compatible with one another?
4. Are any of my roles competing with one another (am I competing with myself)? Am I competing with someone else?
5. Have I chosen a role that will make my work more difficult by its very nature?
6. Is there a particular tone, or attitude, that goes with this role I've chosen? Is it one I really want? Does it fit with who I am as a person?

Deciding the answers to questions about basic values and roles, in yourself, is a necessary first step to being able to make change and growth in anything you do. For some people, asking themselves these kinds of questions is an everyday process. For others, even thinking about such things pushes them outside of familiar, comfortable, territory. That's all right. If you find that these questions make you feel uncertain about your thinking, your orientation toward your work or other people, or even about your basic intentions or true identity, that's good. It means you're thinking; and considering what is best for you and others. If you keep at it, and go at your own pace, you'll find the rewards can be astonishing.

There are a great many people who define themselves by their actions, and will readily define you by yours. Resist this notion as one that defines, and therefore *confines*, people into unnatural and insulting categories. Rather, define yourself as the person you wish to be, then act accordingly whenever possible. When you find yourself "acting out of character", change your actions, your behavior. Don't redefine your character (who you are), and don't let others, unless you've decided you need to make a change on that level. It shouldn't happen very often.

Obviously the questions in this chapter are meant to move you to take some action, now, to make changes. I truly believe in change. There are certainly times when it is best to wait, and react to events as they happen. But more often than not, the waiting makes the problem worse, or even becomes a problem all by itself. Truly successful people seem to be more "proactive" rather than reactive, or at least know which is appropriate, and when. This allows them to move toward what they want, rather than only moving because they need to "get out of the line of fire". In the next chapter you'll begin to decide where you really want to go.

CHAPTER 2

Purpose

Sometimes people focus too much on the problems they are having, and are therefore unable to see the ultimate results that they want. When you think about it, it becomes obvious that solving problems is only important in relationship to the goals and aspirations we have. This is equally true in business or personal affairs. Goal clarification (or even goal setting in some cases), should be a natural and automatic part of all problem solving. Intention and Purpose are central to moving forward toward any solution.

Before that, however, there are some necessary things we need to have in order to effectively solve problems, make decisions, and move toward a goal. First we must believe that our goal is really worthwhile, and possible. We have to want it enough to be motivated to action. Second, we have to have the means to achieve the goal, whether that means knowledge, skill, or other resources. Third, we have to have the opportunity to go after the goal and overcome any resistances that may arise. At the risk of sounding like a detective show on television, these three necessary components to achieving goals can be summarized as:

Motivation (Want to)
Means (How to)
Opportunity (Chance to)

Appreciating our unconscious processes can help us at least as much as appreciating the more usual, tangible, resources at our disposal. It's important to keep in mind that our goals and desired outcomes are not really limited by what we consciously believe we can actually do or achieve. The major limits are in our thinking itself. So, when deciding on a goal, it is best to do so without any immediate regard to whether or not it is "realistic". Once you have gone through these problem solving techniques and processes, that word may have a very different meaning for you.

Well-Formed Outcomes

One way to focus our attention and abilities on achieving goals, or outcomes, is to be able to clearly state, in a sentence if possible, exactly what we want. If this is done in terms of the following five criteria, we can generally insure that we have the motivation, means, and opportunity. These five criteria constitute a framework, or set of guidelines for defining well-formed outcomes.

1. The outcome is **stated in positive** terms.

The outcome must be stated in terms of what you *want*–not what you *don't want*. Watch out for words indicating negation such as don't, won't, shouldn't, can't, stop, etc. Remember negation ("no") does not exist in experience, it only exists in language; just a shorthand to make communication quicker, not more effective.

For example, you could say to yourself: "I don't want any more of these problems we've been having." It's perfectly natural and just about anyone would know what you meant. But how would anyone, including you, be sure exactly what you *did* want instead? A better statement would be: "I want us to move more efficiently and effectively toward our goals than we have been lately." As vague as that statement is, it at least says what you do want, rather than what you don't. It also moves you in a forward direction, toward goals, instead of just away from problems (whatever direction *that* is.)

2. The outcome is **applied to yourself**.

You must focus on what you can do, and be responsible for, not others. It needs to be under your control, or you have no control. Even if the outcome involves others, you can only be sure of how *you* will behave, and, from that, only predict how those actions may effect what others do or think. Of course if a whole team is willing to take on the responsibility for the outcome, then each member becomes part of the solution.

Remember, it is always tempting to notice the shortcomings of others, accurate or not. It is then equally tempting to choose how you would like them to be instead. But how do you get them that way? The only way is to take some action on your own. This may mean confronting them directly, but there may be much better ways. Often, if you make some change in your behavior, or attitude, people around you will automatically change theirs. This is built into the way people, and really all functioning systems, operate (inside and with others). Regardless, the focus of change, and the responsibility for it, must begin with you–then spread to those around you.

3. The outcome is *readily verifiable in sensory terms*.

Make sure you can see, hear, or feel the results of your actions, and the outcome itself. An outcome or goal needs to be specific. A nebulous outcome may keep you from decisive, well directed action.

Even in the last example of a change in "attitude", it is difficult to know when it has happened. A change in your own attitude is only apparent because you *feel* differently, or find yourself *acting* in ways that are new. When you're deciding on a change, it is better to say that you want to feel a different, specific and identifiable, way, than to say you want a new attitude. Then you either feel that way or you don't, and you'll know if you got what you wanted

The same is true of even seemingly well stated goals and outcomes–ones that don't involve feelings and thoughts. If someone says they want to increase income, productivity, their client base or customers, or anything else, it's helpful to set firm targets. The same with decreasing complaints, defects or defections. People really do respond to clearly stated targets by shooting at them. Give dollar amounts, numbers, dates, percentages or other specific measurements, and people will know what to do. They'll also know how well they're doing while they're in the process. This is equally true for yourself.

4. The outcome is *placed in the proper context*.

Make sure you change or produce an outcome, or even any specific behavior, only when and where it will have the desired effect(s), and not in inappropriate situations. A well-formed outcome is specific in form (what), as above, and also in context (where, when and with whom).

The importance of this is especially noticeable in interpersonal relationships. It may be that you, or someone you know needs to be more assertive with others (or a great deal less for that matter). The important thing to remember is that the change may only be needed in certain contexts. For example, you may need to be more active, or even aggressive in selling your ideas to your co-workers or management, but not with your customers. So a goal of "being more forceful" could be perfect in the office but lousy out in the field. Better would be to state it: "Be more direct in getting my ideas across to the *specific* people making the decision on *this* project." Then you know with whom, when, and where to be that way.

5.   The outcome **maintains the positive by-products of previous situations and behavior**.

Sometimes even problem behaviors or situations are doing some good. It is important not to throw out that good effect, while trying to improve the situation and solve problems. Also, it is wise to check through all the possible ramifications of achieving the outcome (or solving the problem), and the behavior leading to it. This will insure that new and unforeseen problems, or unfortunate consequences, aren't created as well.

The last example of being more assertive or direct is a good onc. It could be that a low profile, or even downright passivity, has been good for you for some things. It may even have kept potential conflict and trouble to a minimum. So learning to be more forceful, in a way that *continues* to circumvent conflict (or outright war) could be a real good thing. There are certainly people who manage to assert themselves gracefully and intelligently, and get what they think is best for all concerned, as well.

Another good example is in dealing with any kind of client or customer. Perhaps your style of advertising, marketing, direct support or contact with customers has been of great benefit in keeping the ones you have, and in keeping them satisfied. Changing any of these things to get more customers could be fine, as long as it doesn't insult, or in some way alienate those good and loyal ones you worked so hard for. Balancing these varying needs is as much an art as a science. *Not* balancing them can spell BIG TROUBLE (if this sounds like an example from the "voice of experience" there is a good reason ...).

The above examples of how to follow the guidelines are only some common ones to illustrate the point. The best way to ingrain these ideas in yourself is to practice with your own goals and objectives until you follow the guidelines automatically. And you can really help *others* become more focused in doing so too. Just be sure that you know who to help, how you personally can be of help, why it's a good idea in the first place, and what specifically will be different when you do; while preserving or enhancing the relationship you have with this person. Getting the idea?

Remember also, when you are designing a well-formed outcome, it is not important to know *how* you will get it. Rather concentrate on the above guidelines to insure that it is worth having. It can also help to appreciate that there are nearly always a number of ways to get to the outcome you want. Your job, once the outcome is well designed, is to pick the best choice of which path to take, based on your experience, good judgment and the procedures you'll learn later in this book.

Setting well-formed outcomes is not only good practice, it is vital to being able to clearly focus on what we want. In the following exercise you'll have the opportunity to consider whether your current outcome(s) or goal(s) meets these guidelines.

EXPERIMENT: DESIGNING WELL-FORMED OUTCOMES

Step 1:

Decide on a particular outcome you would like to have – possibly as a result of solving a problem you have. Make this something that you think should happen in the next few weeks or months. Write this outcome, as you state it yourself now, on the lines below or on a separate piece of paper to be used for this exercise.

ORIGINAL OUTCOME:_____

_____

Step 2:

Now take a look at each of the guidelines for developing well-formed outcomes, one at a time. At each step, any adjustments that need to be made should be charted on the lines following each description. They're repeated here to help you.

1.   The outcome is **stated in positive** terms.
The outcome must be stated in terms of what you want–not what you don't want.   Watch out for "negative" words (those indicating negation):   don't, won't, shouldn't, can't, stop, etc.
Adjustments:_____

2.   The outcome is **applied to yourself**.
You must focus on what you can do, and be responsible for, not others.
Adjustments:_____

3.   The outcome is **readily verifiable in sensory terms**.
Make sure you can see, hear, or feel the results of your actions, and the outcome itself. Make it specific.
Adjustments:_____

4.   The outcome is **placed in the proper context**.
Make sure you change or produce specific behavior only when and where it is appropriate.   What, where, when, who.
Adjustments:_____

5.   The outcome **maintains the positive by-products of previous situations and behavior**.
Sometimes even problem behavior or situations are doing some good–keep the baby when the bath water goes.
Adjustments:_____

Step 3:

Write the final well-formed outcome, based on any changes you've just made, on the line below.

FINAL OUTCOME:_____

_____

One of the main things to remember, each time you choose an outcome, or set a goal for yourself, is to be sure that it conforms to your personal standards, and wider values, as a person. It is easy to choose some short term goal that conflicts with the direction you've chosen in your life. Many people, for example, will choose a particular job, or work project, that will make money, satisfy others, or help them appear to be successful, without regard to their real talents or desires. Another example is that many people invest in the stock market in *any* company that appears to offer a good return on investments. If they find themselves investing in a company that is a direct competitor to the one they work for, that may be detrimental to them in the long run. More subtly, they may be investing in a company that supports business practices that go against their personal beliefs, such as weapons manufacture, nuclear power, or environmentally unsafe practices. Any time an immediate success is gained at the expense of some value you hold dear, you run the risk of creating a conflict in your life.

Personal Values & Outcomes

Though this book is aimed at helping specifically with business related problems, I have to get a bit personal with you sometimes, like in Chapter 1. After all, I only have access to you and your thinking. So one of my well-formed outcomes is to ask you to do things that will help you clarify that thinking, so that you can then apply it to the things you most need. Many of the problems and conflicts that arise in business are simply external signs of internal conflicts; perhaps between your values and beliefs, and the actions you need to take. One of the secrets to solving, and indeed preventing conflicts and problems in business, is to insure that business goals and values are aligned with *personal* ones. I'm relying on you to insure this, with help of course, so that you can then be sure of the solutions you develop later on. Here is an experiment to help you do that.

EXPERIMENT: BASIC PERSONAL VALUES

Step 1:

On the following lines on the left hand side, or on a separate piece of paper, list up to ten major values you hold to be of great importance. Then put them in order of priority on the lines to the right.

Basic Values   **Order by Priority of Values**

_____   1._____

_____   2._____

_____   3._____

_____   4._____

_____   5._____

_____   6._____

_____   7._____

_____   8._____

_____   9._____

_____   10._____

Step 2:

Now that you have them on paper in front of you, with the chance for careful reflection, make any changes or adjustments you would like on the lines below.

Adjusted Basic Life Values   **Adjusted Priority of Values**

_____   1._____

_____   2._____

_____   3._____

_____   4._____

_____   5._____

_____   6._____

_____   7._____

_____   8._____

_____   9._____

_____   10._____

I've found the following list of questions to be of value at this point. Consider them carefully.

1. Was it easy to recognize your basic values? How about putting them in order of importance?
2. Were you surprised at any of your choices?
3. Did you make any major adjustments? If so, or if not, why?
4. Are you comfortable with your final choices? Can you foresee future changes in either your basic values or their order of priority?

You may have made some major adjustments in your value structure, just from this simple exercise and discussion. Equally possible is that you may not have thought about these for some time, and you may be a very different person from the one who originally learned, or decided on, them. Most of us change as we grow and learn, but unless we thoughtfully consider changes in our values, we may not make changes that are appropriate in our current lives. Even though we consider ourselves to be consistent in our views, when we think about our immediate and long term goals in light of our basic values, we may find conflicts. This is more a fact of modern life than a serious moral dilemma. The best most of us can hope for is to stay alert to our values, conscious of who we are as individuals, while making strides toward specific goals. Then, if serious conflicts arise, we can use our basic values as a guide in making the tough decisions.

Values in Business

There is also the notion of business values, and *mission*, to consider. Most well run businesses have a clearly stated mission–a purpose for being in business. Some even have a list of purposes, or intentions and a stated *vision*. Even if you are in business for yourself it is a good idea to have a clearly stated mission, based on values you hold dear. It is, in that sense, easier if you run your own business, since you get to choose the values of your business. Either way, it's a good idea to look at your company mission in light of your own values. Here is the same experiment as the one above, but this time focusing on the values of your business.

EXPERIMENT: BASIC BUSINESS VALUES

Step 1:

On the following lines on the left hand side, list up to ten major values you, or your company, hold to be of great importance in business. Then, again, put them in order of priority on the lines to the right or a separate page.

	Order by
Basic Business Values	Priority of Business Values
_____	1._____
_____	2._____
_____	3._____
_____	4._____
_____	5._____
_____	6._____
_____	7._____
_____	8._____
_____	9._____
_____	10._____

Step 2:

Now that you have them on paper in front of you, with the chance for careful reflection, make any changes or adjustments you would like on the lines below.

	Adjusted
Adjusted Business Values	Priority of Business Values
_____	1._____
_____	2._____
_____	3._____
_____	4._____
_____	5._____
_____	6._____
_____	7._____
_____	8._____
_____	9._____
_____	10._____

Step 3:

Now it's helpful to compare the two lists of adjusted values you have, by priority: both your basic personal values and your basic business values (whether these are your own, the ones given to you in your company, or a combination.)

Adjusted *Personal* Values	Adjusted *Business* Values
1._____	1._____
2._____	2._____
3._____	3._____
4._____	4._____
5._____	5._____
6._____	6._____
7._____	7._____
8._____	8._____
9._____	9._____
10._____	10._____

Now answer, for yourself, this list of questions.

1. As you look at these two lists, do you see any basic conflicts between them?
2. If conflicts between your personal and business values and needs have arisen in the past, how have you resolved them?
3. Do you automatically assign one of these sets of values more weight or importance than the other? Which? How did you make the decision about importance, and are you sure you want to keep it that way?
4. Are you comfortable with this final set of lists? Can you foresee future changes in either your basic values, your business values, or their order of priority?
5. How do you perceive, or imagine these values affecting, or creating things you experience as problems in your work?
6. Can you imagine, in the light of the identity vs. role issues we discussed in Chapter 1, that you need to focus more intently on who you are, or wish to be, as a person?

I imagine that going through this exercise has helped clarify, for you, what you are in the business of–your purpose or mission, on both an organizational and a personal level. I certainly intended it that way. If you discovered conflicts you weren't previously aware of, even better. Now you have the opportunity to consider some of these fundamental questions in more depth and with greater clarity of thinking. Remember, though, even if you found conflicts you think are insurmountable, they aren't. It just may take some good creative problem solving to get you over the top.

Alignment of Outcomes

Obviously, even though conflicts in values can cause many problems, there are even simpler kinds of conflicts that can get in your way. In fact, some goals can get in the way of others. For example, taking a job that pays the amount you want may help you in your immediate future. But if you intend to live in another part of the country, and this job holds you where you are, it may not be a wise decision in the long run. This isn't really a question of basic values. More, it's one of planning and aligning of goals and outcomes themselves. People who are successful generally think about the effects of their decisions in terms of long term global goals and outcomes, as well as of immediate future gains. If you have ultimate goals clearly in mind, it is much easier to align short term individual outcomes with your long term vision.

In this next experiment, you'll get to state a long term business goal or outcome you would like to achieve. You'll use the outcome guidelines above, in exactly the way you did before. They are again repeated for you here, without the description of each one. If you need to look back to refresh your memory, feel free. But, hopefully, you now know what each of these criteria mean and how to use them effectively. Going through this process again should help you to internalize these steps and make them more automatic.

EXPERIMENT: ALIGNING WELL-FORMED OUTCOMES

ORIGINAL LONG TERM OUTCOME: _____

_____

1. The outcome is *stated in positive* terms
Adjustments:_____

_____

2. The outcome is *applied to yourself*
Adjustments:_____

_____

3. The outcome is *readily verifiable in sensory terms*
Adjustments:_____

_____

4. The outcome is *placed in the proper context*
Adjustments:_____

_____

5. The outcome *maintains the positive by-products of previous situations and behavior*
Adjustments:_____

_____

FINAL LONG TERM OUTCOME:_____

_____

Now look at the two outcomes you have developed, the first one which will occur in the next few weeks or months, and the second, which is a long term goal. Write them overleaf or on a separate page.

FINAL SHORT TERM OUTCOME:_____

_____

FINAL LONG TERM OUTCOME:_____

_____

Here are some useful questions to ask yourself about these two outcomes.

1.   Are these two outcomes compatible?
2.   If they are, fine. If not, what changes should be made?
3.   What intermediate steps can you imagine that will take you from the first outcome to the second? Are these steps all compatible with each other and the long term goal itself?

It may also be useful to recall a negative example for yourself. Can you think of a time in your past when you set a goal, achieved it, and later decided it was a lousy idea in the first place? Most of us have. This is usually a sign that our short term and long term goals were not compatible in some way, or that any of our goals or outcomes were in conflict (either with themselves or our basic values). Going through the above exercises periodically can prevent the wasted time and energy involved in achieving goals that aren't worth having.

In addition, it is important to consider the results of our outcomes. In other words, when we achieve the goal, will we really have gotten somewhere worth going for who we are as individual people? This is the time to relate goals, outcomes and results to our personal identities–who we really are. I have had many experiences in working with people, in which there were unconscious intentions underlying the more obvious surface level goals these people set for themselves. This is so much a part of the way most of us work that it becomes as invisible to us as water is to a fish. Here are a few questions to ask yourself about your basic intentions; purposely phrased so that you can read them out loud to yourself, and then answer.

1. Is it possible that I may have hidden intentions under-lying my stated purpose or outcome? Are they personal, business, professional, or something else? For example:

   Could I be trying to impress someone? If so, is this the best way to do it?

   Am I trying to develop or enhance a particular relation-ship with someone, in achieving this? Is this a good way to do that?

   Am I simply trying to avoid something else by focusing on, and accomplishing, this? Is that other thing more worthwhile spending my time and energy on directly?

   Am I attempting to create a certain attitude, feeling, or other experience in myself, or in someone else by going after this goal? Is this relevant?

   Am I really trying to get someone else to do something that they don't want to do, or is against that person's nature, in solving this problem or accomplishing this goal?

2. Is it possible that I have too many purposes, or that I've bitten off too large a chunk to chew? Do I need to subdivide the purpose? How? How many purposes do I have? Have I listed these by priority? Are they compatible with one another?

3. Am I the right person to be making these decisions?

4. Can I fully imagine what it would look, sound, and feel like if I actually accomplished my purpose(s)?

5. Have I considered any other possible results or conse-quences of accomplishing this? Is it still worthwhile, after answering these questions?

6. Based on the answers to these questions, do I need to go back through my guidelines for well-formed outcomes and start over, or make some adjustments to what I've already decided on?

Even though I haven't asked you to do so here, you can apply these guidelines for well-formed outcomes, and these questions, to any area of your personal or professional life. Keep them handy. You may even find that doing so helps prevent conflicts or problems arising between personal goals, between personal and work goals, or even between your identity as a person and the role you choose to play at work.

A final comment is in order. There are many ways of setting goals or outcomes for yourself. These guidelines are pretty generic, and you will see some of them repeated in lots of other good books and programs on setting goals. If you have another method that works for you, please, continue to use it. You may find that it complements what you have right here quite well. Also, you may find that this is something you did at one time in your life, and have gotten away from, for whatever reason. If reading this gets you back to good goal setting and planning, then that is certainly worthwhile. You may even find that, as was the case in going through our presuppositions, this alone has helped you solve some problems. If so, congratulations. If not, it will simply become part of the larger process we continue together with the next chapter.

CHAPTER 3

Audience

The question now, once you've considered who you are, your role in solving your problems, and what precisely you want, is: "Who else is involved?" This may seem almost too obvious a point to bring up, but there are some good ways of insuring that you consider those around you, and hopefully, ways of including them within your solutions. The aim is to help you design solutions that are good for everyone involved as well as your business as a whole.

Determining Who is in the Audience

First, you want to consider how many people are involved in the immediate problem itself. Once you have determined this, you need to ask yourself some questions about them, like the ones you asked about yourself earlier. For example, do these others also believe they have the motivation, means, and opportunity to affect any sort of change in the current situation? If not, they will act as if their hands are tied, just as you would in that position. How have you communicated to them about the problem? Do they even know that you consider them to be a part of it? Or even that there is a problem to begin with? These are the fundamental questions that precede any meaningful involvement of others in developing or carrying out any solution or change.

Also, the question arises, "Who will be *affected by* any solutions or changes you try to implement? This could be, conceivably, everyone in the business, suppliers, customers, the community, your family and the families of others as well. This isn't necessarily as grandiose as it sounds. If you think it is, you may not have considered how we affect each other in the systems we live and work in; not to mention how those systems affect each other. Change nearly always creates ripples that travel much farther out than the immediate puddle we dropped the pebble in.

We also have the question, "Who may be *watching* this situation or who might see or hear about the results of whatever you do?" This could be others inside your business, or others outside who have an interest in knowing. Thinking about the community, industry and politics of the situation may give you some clues.

First of all, we need to explore which individuals in your business are directly involved in the problem or any potential solution. Even though we might not have a solution at this point, it may be that you can predict who would need to be a part of one when it is developed. These questions should help in this initial phase:

1. Who do you now think is involved? Can you list them?
2. Do you know what kind of inclusion they need in your planning?
3. Who are they in your business/system? Employees? Co-workers? Superiors? Customers? Suppliers? Outside organization members? Others?
4. Who is *affected* by the problem or situation? Because of this, do they need or deserve to be included in your planning?
5. Who will (maybe only eventually) know about what happens? Do they need to be involved, notified, avoided or in some other way considered as you plan solutions?

Once you have an initial list of individuals you believe are directly involved, it's wise to consider how each person affects the problem, and who else they affect as well. The relationships of people within the system are usually of paramount consideration in planning and making changes. This, of course, includes their relationship with you. For each person you believe is involved, ask the following list of questions:

1. Does this person contribute directly to the problem, or do they affect someone who does? What and who do they affect? In other words, what relationships to others does this person have that could be affecting this problem, or its solution?
2. If you ignored this person, or their input, how would they react? How would others react?
3. Thinking back to when you believe this problem began, was this person directly or indirectly involved?

4. Can you "map out", on paper, the key relationships that are involved in this problem, or could be involved in a solution (sometimes a visual image–an actual picture–can help you recognize the way these interactions affect the situation)?

Once you have an idea about who is involved, and how they affect the problem and one another, it is a good idea to figure out how you might want to include them in thinking about solutions. Sometimes just realizing who they are, and the relationships that exist, can tell you a great deal about changes you might wish to make. Even better, sometimes it shows you exactly how the problem was created. Try the following questions out in clarifying what changes you may want to make regarding the people involved. Again, go through these questions as many times as you need to, in order to ask *each* question in regard to *each* person involved.

1. What kind of inclusion does this person need in your planning?
2. If you were to create some change(s) in this person's behavior, what would it (they) be? Would this person agree that this is a worthwhile change?
3. Would this affect the situation itself? How? Would this person want this change in the situation too?
4. Do you know how you would go about producing these changes (discussions, incentives, training, etc.)?

Now it's time to consider the way the system itself functions, in light of the people you think are affecting this problem. In other words, you need to consider the way your business runs, and how it may be affected in other ways (besides solving this problem or achieving this goal), simply because of the people you have chosen to involve. Also, you need to ask how other systems (other businesses, clients or customers, competitors, suppliers, neighbors and so on) will be affected. Or how they could affect yours.

1. Have you considered how your system functions in terms of who should be included?
2. Have you considered the effects on the system as a whole of including the particular people you've chosen? How about the ones you've excluded?

3. Have you thought about all the other systems your business comes into contact with, in relationship to this problem? In relationship to the particular people you think are involved in the problem?
4. Which people from other systems, outside your business, do you think could be having a direct bearing on this problem? How about on any solutions?

After going through these questions, are there other people you think you need to consider? Are there questions you would like to ask any of these people? When will you ask them? How will you do it in a way that helps everyone involved? These questions move us forward to considering how you communicate with others and how that can help or hinder what you are trying to accomplish.

Communicating With Your Audience

To have any of this make sense, you must consider the wants and needs of all the people involved in any changes you consider implementing. Also, their abilities, working and communicating styles. In fact, if you consider how best to communicate with the other people occupying the problem space along with you, many of the ripple effects may take care of themselves. At the very least, you may have the opportunity to design the *pattern* the ripples take as they spread out.

One way to begin considering and structuring your communication to others in the problem space is to ask yourself at least as many fundamental questions, about them, as you did about yourself when you defined your role. For example, you might want to ask yourself about the basic presuppositions of the people involved. You may not have a good opportunity to ask them all of the questions you would like in determining this, but you would be surprised how much you can estimate, based on your experiences with people.

One note is in order before you begin this process, though. It is very easy to misjudge people when we have strong feelings, positive or negative, about them. We all know this intuitively, but we often forget it during times of stress. If you are angry at someone, or have a vested interest in seeing them do particularly well, or particularly badly, you must detach yourself from these feelings to be able to make an honest assessment of who they really are as people (if this is difficult for you now, you'll learn some new ways later in the book).

Another approach is to take the presuppositions you looked at earlier, and apply them to your *relationship* with this person. For instance, if you take the presupposition that all of their behavior has some positive intention, then it will force you to see them in the light of this intention. Then ask yourself what this intention might be, and how it is affecting their behavior. The same goes for the presupposition that this person has all the resources they really need. From that standpoint, if you want to help them change, the best way to begin is to ask yourself how best to help them get in touch with their own best abilities, talents and internal resources.

RELATIONSHIP AND TASK

A dilemma that many of us have to continually wrestle with lies in balancing the tasks we need to accomplish with the relationships of those we are working with to achieve them. Perhaps the most useful way to deal with this is to remember that unless we have adequate rapport, good relationships, with others, they aren't likely to contribute to our solutions. In fact, they may be part or all of the problem.

On a deeper level we all know this. A connection to other people is a basic need for just about everyone. We are social beings and we need others to accomplish most of our goals in work and in life. It can be frustrating to have to spend so much time on these social needs, especially when we are focused on our goals. However, to be truly successful, we need to broaden that focus. We need to keep other people, and our relationship with them, in mind.

One way I've found helpful is to remember the *order* in which we do things when we are dealing with others. Sales professionals (and everyone in the influence business) know this. They know that the first goal they have with any prospective client or customer is to establish understanding and trust: in other words, rapport. They need to have that as a basis of all their communication. We sometimes call this the "rapport frame". Without it, they get nothing accomplished. So most sales training is focused to a large extent on relationship to the client first, selling the service or product second.

This focus should be the same any time we have new ideas or recommendations to present to those we work with. Relationship first, task second. This, by the way, should also be the basis of all the relationships in our lives, not just in business.

Perhaps as important is to remember that the meaning of any of your communications is the response that they elicit *–regardless of what you intended.* Perhaps when you think back on how you've been communicating, the behavior that you've seen in those around you begins to make perfect sense. It may take some time, flexibility, and honesty with yourself to notice this. In fact, it may take remembering that all you really need to notice it is: truly open channels of communication and the awareness to perceive the results of your actions.

Beyond that, it is always possible that your rapport with those around you is not what it should be. If people you work with don't trust you, or even understand you very well, they certainly won't do what you want (at least not simply because you want them to). On the other hand, maybe they do trust and understand you, but have legitimate objections or concerns you haven't dealt with. All of these possibilities come under the heading of good communication. They are necessary for you to get full fledged cooperation and enthusiasm from the people you work with.

I hope you are getting used to the idea of considering your basic presuppositions, and those of others, when trying to initiate any kind of change. Before you can make a change, you need to know where you are starting from. These presuppositions are the most basic starting place to consider. It is worth taking another look over Chapter 1 if the answers to any of the above questions and possibilities leads you to believe that they could be the source of your difficulties. Without having some sense of alignment at this most basic level, you might not get too far.

Next is to ask yourself what the primary purpose(s) of the other people you are dealing with might be. Also, what may be secondary purposes, just as you did with yourself. If these purposes are in direct opposition to yours, or in some way incompatible, you may need to do some negotiation about it. Perhaps these people have multiple purposes that are in conflict with each other, and this affects their behavior in some way. In fact, it may well be that you are dealing with several people who are in conflict with one another. Handling that may be your biggest task.

Individual characteristics

This leads us to the notion of the individual personality traits or characteristics of everyone involved in the problem space. These could become important in making the necessary changes to improve the situation. In business in the past few years it has become popular to apply one of several personality style "inventories" to analyze, and categorize, employees or customers. The reason this is popular is because it helps.

These tests and inventories are used, of course, strictly for business purposes. Most of the people who use them have no particular interest in the psychological make-up or problems of the people they assess. Rather we use these tools to help people understand the best ways to work with each other. They can also be helpful in knowing the best ways to approach customers. You don't usually have the opportunity to use these inventories on everyone you work with, but thinking about the possible variables involved, along with what you do know, can help you shape the information you want to present. You may have good information from previous contacts you have had. You may learn something from others whose judgment you trust. You can even make some predictions about people you haven't had contact with if you know *some* information about them; but this, of course, is risky.

The particular inventory we use in NLP is called Sorting Styles. It is based on the internal information processing and filtering categories called Meta-Programs that I mentioned earlier. You don't need to understand how these really work to use them. They are simply tendencies we all have toward noticing different things, responding to them, and organizing our thinking and experience. More than anything else, these describe an *orientation* a person may take. And, like all inventories of this type, they work most accurately when applied to a particular situation. The presuppositions we've been discussing show basic beliefs and assumptions that people have. These Sorting Styles show how people actually *operate* in their interactions and dealings with others. This can include what motivates them, how they make decisions, what they pay attention to, and how they may handle certain kinds of situations.

Because these "programs" affect our motivation, decision making, and behavior toward others, knowing how they operate in those we work with can help us communicate and work with them much more effectively. Rather than describe them in detail, which isn't necessary, I'll simply ask you a number of questions about the person you're working with, and you can either answer directly, or make your best assumptions. Hopefully you will base these judgments on some good observations. We call this *evidence*.

If you really haven't any observations that can provide you with this information, it doesn't mean all is lost. You can always take a "generalized" approach when communicating with people. For example, as you'll see below, some people respond primarily to avoid trouble, others to find new opportunities. Some sales people, when meeting clients for the first time, present information that will appeal to both. A savvy salesperson might show the possible results of missing the opportunity to have their product or service, while simultaneously pointing out the benefits of having it. It is a good idea to try to cover as many bases like this as feasible within each category, or set of questions, so that you can find out what works with people. That way you'll be likely to hit your mark. So have these ideas in mind when you approach these people the next time, and ask yourself the questions again then.

By the way, these are equally valid to ask about yourself. Remember, the answers change when you ask them about different things. You can't really categorize people in some blanket way using this set of ideas. They show tendencies toward perceiving, thinking and acting *in specific contexts*. For example, you will be different at work from how you are at home with your family, or on vacation in another part of the world. You may be different working on your bookkeeping than at a board meeting; different on the phone with a client than working out a problem with co-workers. Try and keep the specific problem or goal you are working on in clear focus while you think about the people involved.

As you look at each question, think about past experiences with the person you are answering the question about, or yourself. If you can come up with specific examples of how they handled similar situations to the one you are in now, in relation to each of the categories, you should be able to get a good overall picture of how they generally behave in this kind of situation. Remember though, these are just generalizations. That means there may be exceptions to all of the answers you come up with and these exceptions may apply to the present circumstances you find yourself in.

Each question is phrased as though you were going to present a proposal, or some idea or information to someone. Pick one of the people on your list and imagine that you have to do that to get them to participate in helping you solve this problem. Then repeat it with each of the other people involved. Here are your questions:

Convincers

1. What convinces this person of the value of something? Do they rely on what is in front of them, here and now, or do they need to see results over a **TIME PERIOD**? How long a time period would be necessary to convince this person, or group of people, of the worth of your ideas?
2. Are they more likely to pay attention to **PAST** experiences, **PRESENT** contacts and presentations, or the promise of **FUTURE** benefits, services or guarantees?
3. Would they need to see a certain **NUMBER** of successes, **EXAMPLES** of positive experiences, to make a judgment, perhaps independent of how much time it takes?
4. In making their judgments, would they need to **SEE** results, or **READ** reports of effectiveness? Would they need to **HEAR** from other people who have had experience with you or what you propose? Would they need their own **EXPERIENCE**, say a trial run or sample of some sort? Do they have to "**FEEL** it's right".
5. How about the five great questions: Who, What, Where, When, or How–to convince this person of what you propose?

Motivators

1. Is the person you are dealing with more likely to be **PROACTIVE** or **REACTIVE**? In other words will this person be likely, or even able, to act on his or her own initiative? Is he or she more likely to wait for something to happen, and then respond (*act*, or *react*)?

2. The most important question may be, can this person act at all, or does he or she have to wait for *someone else* to make a decision? Depending on the answer to that question, are you certain, right now, that you are dealing with the right person?

3. Assuming that this is the right person, or one of the right people, do they rely heavily on **EXTERNAL** information, that which comes from others to make decisions, or on what they feel and think based on their own **INTERNAL** processes (gut reactions, clearly thought out procedures, values, rules, etc.)? How can you use this information to help both of you achieve your goals?

4. Does this person tend to operate TOWARD pleasure, success and possibility, or **AWAY FROM** pain, and perceived problems? In other words, does he or she respond to fear and punishment (sticks) or pleasure and rewards (carrots)?

5. If you don't know, can you gracefully include both as possibilities in your communication with them? Can you show the negative consequences of not taking your advice or suggestions, while at the same time showing the advantages of following your lead?

6. Will this person respond to your presentation because of the **POSSIBILITIES** involved, or because they perceive they have no other choice, i.e. out of **NECESSITY**?

7. Will this person likely respond to how your products, services, ideas or proposals **MATCH** something he or she is already familiar with? Or, on the other hand, do you need to show how what you offer is a **MISMATCH** for what is expected such as a unique feature of some sort? In other words, does this person look for things that are the **SAME** as something they are already familiar with, or things that are **DIFFERENT**, when making a decision? If you don't know, can you include features of both sameness and difference in what you present?

Thinking Style

1. It is possible to focus one's attention more on small details, or on more general, abstract ideas. Which should you concentrate on? Should you start with **GENERAL** ideas and move toward more SPECIFIC ones in your dealings with this person? Perhaps the other way around? Does this person have to, or need to, "see the big picture" to act on something, or would they rather a series of small steps?

2. Can you list, in **ORDER OF PRIORITY**, the things relevant to your proposal that you think are most important to this person or group of people? How can you organize your thinking, or the content of your presentation, that will respect, appreciate, and, most of all, respond directly to their priorities?

3. Finally, are there some **RULES** that this person chooses, or is forced to follow, in responding to you? How can you make it easy for them to follow these rules while responding favorably to you in the process?

It may have seemed an overwhelming task just to answer a few of these questions. It may, in fact, not even be necessary to do so to accomplish your immediate purpose or solve the problem at hand. In some very important cases, however, wise time spent thinking about these issues and approaches will save you a great deal of wasted time presenting irrelevant ideas. It may also help insure that you have properly targeted your intended audience to get the response you want. I suggest that, if answering this list of questions seems like overkill to you, simply read it over and notice if any of the questions jog some memory or thought that might be of value. That is really what it is intended for.

Ultimately, considering these factors while communicating with others is a sign of respect. It means you care about them, and your goals, enough to take the time and energy to present your ideas to them in the way they can best understand and respond to. Asking these questions about yourself is a sign of self-respect for the same reasons. It also gives you the opportunity to learn more about your own individual characteristics and thinking style, and to make changes.

As in most endeavors, it is important to have a clear image of the individual people, or group of people, you are working with. Be able to see them clearly in your mind, and imagine talking with them, to test what you plan to communicate. With the addition of the answers to the above questions, and a firm purpose in mind, you should be well on your way to working with these other important people. Together you will solve your problems and achieve your goals and outcomes.

CHAPTER 4

Code

The concept of code is an interesting one, and one that is important in understanding how you actually understand your problems and goals. We all code things in our minds. We don't actually think about entire experiences; rather we take "shorthand" versions that we later recall and operate on. These shorthand slices of thinking and experience can disrupt our activities while we try to reach our goals and outcomes. That's because whenever we break something down into a coded form, we have to change it. Sometimes the changes help out, sometimes they cause problems.

Most of us have had the experience of taking a trip, or a vacation even, and coming home with a bunch of snapshots to show our friends and family (if we haven't had the experience, certainly someone has shown us their pictures at some time). The pictures become our shorthand version of the vacation. They certainly don't have the sounds, smells, feelings and tastes that we had, even though they may remind us of them. And they couldn't possibly include more than a tiny percentage of what we actually saw. So when we show them to friends, there is no way they can possibly experience what we did when we were actually there. That's why so many people joke about the horrors of watching someone's home movies of their vacation; it just isn't the same. In some cases, it's hard to imagine how someone could even have had a good time, from watching what they show us.

The three unavoidable information processes

Whenever information is involved, there are three processes that come into play. These are things people always do, to some extent, when they perceive, think about, or communicate something. The three processes are:

Deletion
Distortion
Generalization

These act as filtering mechanisms between what actually happens around us, or to us, and what we *think* has happened. These natural processes affect us whether we're aware of them or not. They're unavoidable.

What this means is that we aren't ever really operating with totally accurate information. When we make decisions we are always working with insufficient, and in some respects inaccurate, information on which to make judgments. Even when we communicate to others, we can't give them everything in our minds exactly the way it is. Maybe we wouldn't want to. From our vacation pictures, for example, we leave some things out (how we *really* looked in our bathing suits), change others (maybe that fish wasn't *quite* that big), and make generalizations about still more (well, maybe the weather wasn't perfect the *whole* time).

These three processes are automatic, even when we perceive the world around us. For example, we can't possibly notice, at least not consciously, all of the information (sights, sounds, feelings, tastes and smells) around us. Even if we could, the sheer quantity would overload all our circuits to the point of a mental meltdown. So, out of sheer self-defense, we ignore most of it: this is deletion. Hopefully, we have learned some useful rules for knowing what is worthwhile to pay attention to and what we can safely let go of. Even if our rules were "perfect", though, what we think is really important can change as quickly as each new situation we wander into.

Once we have figured out what's worth keeping and what isn't, a lot of it still won't fit with what we know or expect. So we make it fit: this is distortion. Ask yourself how many times you've slightly changed what someone told you so that it matched what you wanted it to mean, and you'll understand what I'm talking about. Isn't it interesting how bent out of shape we can get when other people reconstruct our (brilliant, earth-shattering, crucial) concepts to fit their (unimportant, ridiculous, idiotic) needs and ideas?

Beyond that, we have the need to make some consistent sense out of life in general, and our own in particular. So we come up with more rules to organize our thinking: these are generalizations. As we've all discovered, no two people share the same set of generalized beliefs about anything, so we spend a lot of our time arguing about these, based on our most important and relevant experiences. If only we all had the same experiences it would be so much easier. Still, we would delete and distort them in our own unique ways. Our generalizations would come out different from each other anyway. This is what happens when two or more people come out of the same meeting (movie, lecture, class, vacation, whatever) and act as if they had entirely different experiences. They did.

The scariest part of this whole collection of processes is that, with each individual piece of information we try to communicate to someone, we've already gone through these deletions, distortions, and generalizations *at least three times*. The first was when we took in the information originally. Second, when we thought about it, cataloged it, and stored it in our minds. Third, when we changed it into (our own) words so we could say it to someone else. And this doesn't include what our brain did with it in between. It's like an internal version of that kids classroom game called telephone: one person starts a message at one end of the class, and by the time it gets to the other end it no longer even remotely resembles the original. Some of us often wonder how it is possible to make a good decision, effectively solve a problem, or even communicate a simple thought to someone else (who will, of course, do these same things to what we tell them). Yet, amazingly, we seem to get along for the most part.

Belief systems & thought viruses

Throughout our lives we have been gathering information and making judgments about it, through these distortions we've been discussing. These become our generalizations about ourselves, other people and the world as a whole. We call these generalizations *beliefs*. The collection of beliefs that we have as a whole we call our "belief systems". It really is useful to think of sets of beliefs as systems, because they act like systems. They form relationships with one another, affect one another, and affect everything else that has to do with them. In this sense our belief system is much like an air conditioning system with its thermostat, tubing, wiring, sensors, motors, fans and compressor. All of this stuff has to work together to get the job done. The various beliefs act like parts of a system that affect each other, and as a whole affect us. And this includes causing us to suffer when the system breaks down.

These breakdowns are primarily what give us fits. Like any system, our belief systems can break down from outside pressure; conflicting information, for example. They can also break down from internal pressure, conflicting beliefs, internally conflicting information, or some other confusion.

Sometimes, though, the system works absolutely perfectly, like a well oiled machine, and gets us into enormous trouble nevertheless. This can be the result of beliefs that, though consistent, lead us into situations or actions that don't work to get us what we want (or even to keep us out of trouble). Worse, we often give these beliefs to other people who also think, and act as if they are worthwhile and valuable. When this happens, the trouble we give ourselves is then spread and multiplied, like a virus. These "thought viruses" are every bit as dangerous as physical ones (in fact Robert Dilts has successfully demonstrated that they can cause physical problems). In addition, they are equally contagious and difficult to spot. We usually catch them in places where we come in close contact with others, like at home with our families, or at work. We don't usually know we have them until the system itself is suffering severe symptoms. Then they spell trouble.

Relief, in this case, is spelled P-R-E-V-E-N-T-I-O-N. This includes repeatedly asking yourself and those around you the questions I've provided. Who are you, and they. What do you believe. What are you capable of, and so on.

For us, as in all human affairs, it helps to accept all of these natural filtering, communication, and belief processes as part of the cost of living, and doing business. Once we do that, we can learn to recognize and work with them, rather than giving up, or scaring ourselves into hiding in the nearest closet. That is what this concept of code is about: getting along with and overcoming these fundamental, though natural and inevitable, processes in perceiving, thinking, and communicating.

The Seven C's

Determining how you get in your own way–what internal interferences you set up – is one way to analyze how you go about deleting, distorting and generalizing; and making thought viruses. Robert Dilts has a set of organizing principles called "The Seven C's Model". You can think of the Seven C's as the Seven Conundrums, or problems, that you need to *overcome* to have real mental clarity and focus on achieving your goals. This is also an excellent trouble shooting guide for checking yourself on how you are thinking about, or coding, your problem space. Each of these seven processes is a tried and true method for screwing up.

1. **Confusion**. As obvious as the first of The Seven C's sounds, we don't always know that we are confused about something, or what exactly is confusing us. This lack of clarity, or inability to focus, can make a mess of our well thought out plans. It may be, in fact, that our well-formed outcome isn't so well-formed in reality. It is important to have a clear mental image, or even written criteria for knowing we've gotten what we want, in the ways that I described in Chapter 2.

The problem of *smoke screens* are familiar to most of us. We can have our judgement clouded for lots of reasons, and in lots of ways. We often get vague and general when we need to be specific. We can blank out important details, ideas or other information, simply deleting these things from our awareness. We can fool ourselves in a variety of ways to avoid getting in touch with bad feelings we may have about what we need to do. Avoidance usually breeds more problems, which can lead to further avoidance and a descending spiral into a smoky cloud of problems we don't know how to face. Often, when we look back later on the mess we've made, we can clearly see how we fooled ourselves.

Questions:

1. What images do you have in your mind when you think about this problem or situation? Are these images actually clear pictures in your mind?

2. What do you say to yourself, or others, about this problem or situation?
3. How do you feel, when you think about this?
4. Have you had the experience of thinking about this or related problems or situations, and later finding that your perceptions, ideas, or worries were inaccurate?
5. How accurate do you believe the images, things you say, and feelings you have about this situation or problem actually are? Do you have *evidence* to know if you are accurate in your thinking?

2. **Content**. It is always possible to have improper information or materials at hand while you are trying to achieve your goals. The old computer programming maxim "garbage in-garbage out" comes to mind. One of the most common difficulties we manufacture, in this sense, is *red herrings*: truly unimportant or irrelevant details. Chasing these is really a very simple way we can unconsciously fool ourselves and mess up our sense of direction. Knowing which pursuits take us directly toward our desired outcomes is the key to avoiding this trap. We're looking for consistency here; making sure there are no missing links in our chain of information and action.

In a related manner, many of us fall into the trap of spending 80% of our time on the least important 20% of what we need to focus on. Sometimes we know it, but that doesn't really help much unless we *do something about it*. This, again, comes down to consistently facing, and doing, the most important things, no matter how painful, when we need to.

There is an old saying from anthropology and information sciences, generally attributed to anthropologist Gregory Bateson, that goes "information is the difference that makes a difference." But only if it is good information.

Questions:

1. What concrete information do you have about this situation or problem? Is it reliable?
2. How would you know if the information you had was worthwhile or not? Do you have some system in place to double-check what you have? Could you be missing something?

3. Are you sure that what you are focusing on is truly relevant, or the most relevant? Are you consistently spending time on aspects of this that aren't important enough to make a difference?

CHANGING YOUR STORY

Metaphors - stories - are an integral part of life. From a very young age we hear and become a part of the stories we see and hear. And they become a part of us. We learn from them, are enriched and challenged by them, and change as a result of them. This process of taking in and connecting what we hear about others to our own lives is as natural as taking in food as nourishment. We relate to others through our shared stories as much as our shared experiences.

We also use these stories to understand ourselves, just as we use them to understand the world around us. We talk to ourselves inside just about all the time. It helps us to make sense and order in what happens to us and in how we respond to these events. Most of us, in understanding some important event, will make a number of interpretations and conclusions about it. These serve to solidify our understanding of it and to put it into a framework that explains it in the context of our lives. They become our stories.

Story telling is as natural as living. The problem with the process, however, is that our stories tend to become "written in stone" in our minds. They become rigid and limiting. They satisfy our need to have things organized and simple, but limit our flexibility and creativity, often when we most need them.

Being willing to pay close attention to the "story" we tell about whatever problem we are having can help us see how we may have "written ourselves into a corner." This makes sense if you think about times in the past when you have solved an important problem. We almost always end up telling a different story about it after we've successfully tackled it. And that new story becomes the basis for the new beliefs or conclusions we make about the situation in hindsight. Why wait? Maybe if we just re-write the story while we're having the problem, we can overcome it by changing the way we believe it is structured. Change the story to change the problem. The change can work in either order.

3. **Conflict**. Maybe we are unsure about what it is that we really want or need. Or maybe we want something, but some part of us knows it isn't good for us. Or that getting it, in the way we have set out to, in some way conflicts with our beliefs or who we are as individuals. This will cause incongruity in our behavior. We'll think or say one thing, but do another. Also, we could have some real secondary gain in keeping things the way they are (secondary gain means it could be doing us some good *not* to make a change or solve our problem). Perhaps we have an agenda we've hidden from ourselves!

Certainly the same thing can happen with others too. Good communication and understanding will usually lead to some sort of consensus about approach. This will minimize conflict.

Questions:

1. When you think about how you have been going about dealing with this problem or situation up to this point, have you been congruent in your behavior and communication? Or, have you been acting in ways that don't fit with who you are and how you operate?
2. Have others made comments to you about how you've been handling this that lead you to question your own intentions, motivation, or consistency? Do you have conflicts with others that you could clear up and come to some agreement or consensus about?
3. Can you imagine some good or worthwhile outcome, event, or by-product of having this problem or situation *stay as it is*? - for yourself or others?
4. If you were able to make a real change in this situation tomorrow, what *costs*, not just in money, obvious or subtle, would there be?

4. **Catastrophes**. In many ways, we are all a product of our past. That includes the good things, the learning, and the experience we have gathered over our lives and our work. It also, of course, includes the bad things, the ones we have thought of as mistakes, the traumatic experiences that have left scars and the painful memories that we carry with us. To say that "those who don't learn from the past are condemned

to repeat it" is actually quite an understatement. For many of us, failure to learn from our past *amplifies* the problems we get into. This is because the stakes of our activities usually go up as we go forward. They also usually include other peoples' needs besides our own. There may be some things we need to resolve from our past, to have firm conviction and a direction for the future.

Questions:

1. Have you had past experiences that you believe may be affecting your judgment about this one? Perhaps making you uncomfortable, or hesitant to act? Or, worse, causing you to act in ways that will never have any effect?
2. What have you done about this problem or situation in the past?
3. When you think about this problem or situation, what are you reminded of? Are there any memories that have emotional baggage attached to them? Could this be causing additional difficulty (or even be the source of it)?
4. Are you victimizing yourself by always doing what you've always done (and thus always getting what you've always gotten)?

5. **Conviction**. Probably the most damaging and subtle barrier to our success in achieving our goals is our own collection of doubts. Remember motivation, means and opportunity? If we don't have all three, and *believe* we have them, we're likely to sabotage ourselves more effectively than even our most ardent critics. We need to be sure of ourselves, as well as internally congruent, to have real, whole-hearted conviction.

Sometimes, to build our emotional conviction to a high enough level, we need to reach what, in NLP, we call a *critical mass*. Simply, this means that sometimes there are a number of factors that need to occur before a change can be made. For example, as we discussed in Chapter 3, some people are convinced of something because someone they trust tells them it is so. Some people need to be told by a number of people. Some people need to read convincing evidence, some need to see something in action, and some need to try it out for a while. There are those of us, however, who need more than one of the above: sometimes several different kinds of experiences, along with reading a few articles (and the fine print) and talking to others. Until we have compiled *enough* information to convince us (critical mass) nothing will happen. But once we reach that threshold, nothing can stop the chain reaction.

Questions:

1. How is your conviction level? Are you whole-hearted, or only half?
2. Do you need something to convince you that tackling this situation is worth your best efforts? Do you need a collection of things, information or other motivators, to do this (critical mass)? How could you gather this collection together? How would you be sure that you've got it?
3. How would you know, or feel, if you were absolutely determined to solve this problem or make the necessary changes? Different than now?
4. Is there anything (or anyone) else preventing you from being totally committed to reaching your goal?

6. **Context**. External impediments to our goals are always going to exist in some form or another. In fact, they can usually be safely assumed to be a standard part of what we will have to deal with. The environment will do what it does best; provide an ample supply of both obstacles and resources for us to choose from on our journey toward our goals. This is the context in which we all work and live, whether we recognize it or not. Creativity is the tool we have *all* been given to handle the outside world.

Questions:

1. What outside forces have been affecting this situation up to this point?
2. What are some other possible outside influences that could get in the way of your outcome?
3. Could worry about these external factors be affecting your judgment, motivation, or perceptions?

4. Is the environment surrounding this situation one in which you are comfortable operating? Are you knowledgeable, experienced, and capable in this context? Can you tap into your best creativity to deal with any outside forces?

7. **Comparison**. It is easy to take our past experiences and present desires and come up with really inappropriate expectations of (or criteria for) success. Many of us suffer from comparison with others as well. This is usually useless and inappropriate. These comparisons are often based on generalizations and distortions we've made in our minds. Sometimes they provide motivation to us, but more often they result in fear and mis-direction of our energies. So whether we are comparing ourselves to others, comparing our results to some ridiculous standard, or trying to match things up so that everything fits neatly with our expectations, we are wasting our time.

There is an old joke about a crazy psychiatrist who theorizes that everyone's problems are the result of having *fish in their dreams*. So, a man comes in to see the psychiatrist and begins to discuss his problems, only to be interrupted by the doctor asking him about whether he dreams of fish at night. The man says no. The doctor persists by asking if the man dreams of water. Again the man says no. Then the psychiatrist asks if there could be water around anywhere in any dreams. Again, no. Then the doctor asks if it might have rained recently, in the man's dreams, or if there could have been water nearby, at any time, that the man might have missed seeing. The man says he isn't sure, to which the psychiatrist persuades him into believing in the *possibility* of water, somewhere in one of his dreams. Then he gets the man to agree that water could have fish in it. Since there could have been fish, in the water in the dreams that the man wasn't aware of–VOILA! The psychiatrist is completely satisfied, convinced, as always, that the man's problems are caused by the fish in his dreams. Crazy, huh? But how many of us fight just as hard to hold on to the things we believe, no matter how far-fetched? Sometimes it is difficult to deal with a new belief, but remember, the map is not the territory.

By the same token, we often expect others to behave in ways that they can't understand or even know about, because of our own standards and perceptual filters. It is easy to fall into the trap of the "crazy" psychiatrist. Clear communication will help prevent this. It may also keep us out of the psychiatrist's office altogether....

Questions:

1. Are you trying to match (or mismatch) some particular outcome, or set of circumstances in solving this problem? Is this a *valid* or *useful* comparison? How do you know?
2. Are you comparing yourself to someone else, or to some way you were at another time? Is this reasonable? Worthwhile? Helpful?
3. Similarly, are you expecting someone else to match some expectation of yours? Do they know what it is? Have you communicated it effectively?
4. Have you, until now, been attempting to fit this problem or situation into some category that you think you know how to deal with? Does it really fit? Do you "see every problem as a nail, simply because you're holding a hammer?"
5. If someone else, an impartial expert perhaps, were to look at this situation from the outside, would they see this fit the same way you do?

Usually, when we reach a major impasse of some sort, even though we think we know what we want, it is a sign that one of The Seven C's is at work. If we think of each of them as a condition to be overcome before we can really get what we want, we'll be on the lookout for them. Once each has been cleared out, it helps insure that our thinking is cleared up. Then we can proceed toward developing our solutions and, in an organized way, working toward our outcomes. The transformations can look like the chart below.

THE SEVEN C's

Conundrums	——————>	Cures
Confusion	——————>	Clarity
Content	——————>	Consistency
Conflict	——————>	Consensus
Catastrophe	——————>	Conviction
Conviction	——————>	Congruency
Context	——————>	Creativity
Comparison	——————>	Communication

Neuro-Logical Levels

Once you have your thinking about any problem or issue fairly clear, you still have to *organize* your thinking in a way that helps you work toward a solution. The coding you develop for this organization will show you which tools you'll need, both physical and mental, to get the job done. One place to start is in looking at the problem space as a whole. As an aid, we can use Robert Dilts' Neuro-Logical Level categories, based on the work of anthropologist Gregory Bateson and others. These levels can be applied to just about anything you can think of. They form a clearly logical basis for organizing your approach to problem solving and change of all kinds. The following diagram shows the levels. It is followed by an explanation, and a series of questions you can ask, to help you see the relationships between them.

Figure 4

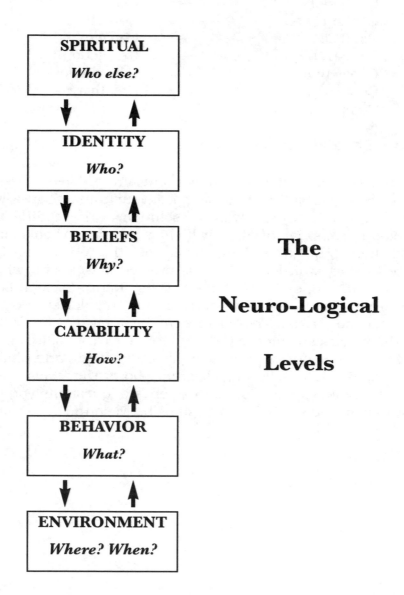

Let's take a good look at this arrangement from the bottom up, starting at the level of environment, because it will make more sense that way.

Environment

A safe and properly designed environment is essential to most projects. For life itself, food, shelter, and security are essential. Solving problems is certainly no exception and, in fact, an unsafe (in any sense of the word) environment may be the source of the problem. Most people need a safe place just to be able to *think* clearly about what it is that they want. This could be a physical location or, in a broader sense, the business environment itself that we are talking about.

It is also important to consider time as well as place. It may be easier and more conducive to take on a task if other things are taken care of first, or if interruptions are anticipated. Though these considerations may seem ridiculously obvious, it's still important to be reminded of them, and be clear about them, at the beginning. I'm continually astonished at how what is obvious to some people can seem so obscure to others (including me). As you can see from the chart, the environmental level is the "where and when" of your problem space. The following questions will help you in thinking about environment in relationship to the other levels of analysis.

Questions:

1. What considerations are there in the physical environment surrounding this problem area?
2. Are there social boundaries? Are there financial, political, or other constraints on potential solutions?
3. Are there any concerns about the environment in which you are operating that could impinge on your thinking, creativity, or motivation in solving this problem or making the changes you need?
4. Will there be any cost to the environment (again, in *every sense* of the word, social, emotional, financial, political, etc.) in which you are operating if you achieve your outcome or goal?

Behavior

Next we have the behavioral level. This includes thoughts and feelings, as well as all the other activities associated with doing something, in our case working toward a solution to our problems. For example, many people get quite nervous when they think about what they have to do. The nervousness is a behavior, and one that will cancel out the value of a whole lot of other behaviors. In addition to controlling thoughts and feelings, there will be many small tasks involved, from deciding what to do at the beginning, to organizing, and carrying through to a finished product or goal. This is the "what" to do.

Questions:

1. How are you handling any feelings you may have about this problem? What do you say to yourself or others about it? Does this affect the situation?
2. Do you feel guilty, or blame yourself for this situation or problem? How does this affect you?
3. How do you see the situation, from your perspective? How does this compare to the perspective of others?
4. How have you acted to solve this so far? Perhaps most importantly, what have you *avoided* doing? Why?

Capability

Next we come to the level of capability, the "how" in any task. Obviously it is possible to have the environment arranged perfectly, and to know exactly *what* has to be done to accomplish the task, but to have no earthly idea *how* to do it. "How" means capability, processes, procedures, strategies. Though we'll get to methods for developing solutions and carrying them out later, there are still good questions that need to be answered now.

Questions:

1. Do you know, at this point, what you need to *be able* to do to affect this problem or achieve your outcome?
2. Realistically, what are your capabilities as a person? What are they in relationship to this problem?

3. Have you exercised your true capabilities so far? If not, do you know why, or what you have to do differently?
4. How do you go about developing and improving your capabilities?

Beliefs

No matter how much you know, and how capable you are, you may still not believe in your abilities, or value their worth. If this is the case, you *won't* be likely to *use* your abilities, even if you can. This is the logical level of beliefs and values, or "why" you should do anything.

Remember those thought viruses I mentioned earlier? Perhaps you're one of the many people who lost confidence in yourself at some point in your life or career. Maybe you had help, in this loss of confidence, from school, peers, family, or some other, even well intentioned but ultimately defeating, outside force. Now maybe you've "internalized" this negative attitude so you no longer try. If this is the case, you're in luck. It turns out that most people who have shattered self-confidence can rebuild their belief in themselves with just a little practice.

Questions:

1. What do you believe about this problem? About yourself?
2. Do you believe you are at fault, or that you created this situation? Do you believe someone else is at fault (and do they know that you feel this way)? If so, how do you think you have affected yourself (or others) with these beliefs?
3. Do you carry negative, limiting beliefs around with you in other areas of your life? If so, can you remember where you learned them?
4. Do you believe you can solve this problem? Do you believe anyone can–that it can be solved at all?
5. Do you believe you need to do it alone? With the help or advice of others? Do you believe you are capable?

Identity

The sum of your behaviors, your capabilities and your beliefs is your identity: "who" you are, in anything that you do. Chapter 1 was designed to help you get a handle on this. But it is worthwhile to think about all of those same things again, in the light of these other levels. This is so especially now that you've thought about so many other related issues. Without a firm identity you can easily flounder. Make sure you are congruent, consistent within yourself, while you take on your problems.

Questions:

1. Who are you–from your own perspective? From the perspective of others?
2. How does this problem affect or involve you? How do you affect it?
3. What is your role or responsibility in this sense. Is this truly *your* problem? Would it be best left, or given, to others?
4. Do you believe that having this problem says something about who you are as a person?

Spiritual

Finally, we have the spiritual level of analysis. This means how you are connected to the world outside of yourself. The word "spiritual" here does not necessarily have anything to do with a religious sense of the word, but it could if you choose. More, it means "who else" is involved with you, your identity, your beliefs, capabilities, and behaviors. In business this is especially important. None of us operates in a vacuum. We are connected to others somehow, in our wider circles of community, industry, country and the world. If we remain aware of that connection, and use it in effective ways, we'll certainly be much better off. We'll probably be better people, as well.

Questions:

1. Who else is involved besides you? Who else is affected besides you? How "wide" is this effect?
2. Who else would care about this, regardless of their involvement or whether it affects them?
3. Is there someone you are thinking about in this way, that perhaps you have not been fully conscious of until now?
4. Who besides you would have to pay some price if you achieved your outcome? In considering this, does it affect your thinking, judgment, motivation or beliefs? How have you communicated this to others?
5. If there will there be effects in your wider circles of influence (community, industry, country and the world) if you achieved your outcomes, are these ones you can be proud of?

Obviously you've answered some of these questions before, in Chapter 3, but again, it is useful to think in terms of the Neuro-Logical Levels when thinking about who is really involved. This helps make sure that our problem space is clear so that we can know how to proceed.

One of the things I stressed at the beginning of this book was that I would take you through many thoughts about problem solving, over and over, and from different angles. Systems don't work in one linear direction. They work in circles. Interconnections. Relationships. The way to understand them is to observe one part working, and watch how the other parts respond. The same is true in what we're trying to accomplish here. Each time you make a change, a decision, an agreement, or any communication, every other part of your system–your life and your business–will be affected. That means you are never really finished asking these questions. Because each time you answer one, it affects all the others that follow it, and the ones that came before as well.

These questions are meant not only to help you see and hear through your perceptual filters, but to change the filters themselves. If you take control of the filtering process, and understand the information you take in better and more clearly, it can only help you affect your system in ways that will move you toward your goals. You may find, as you ask these questions over and over, that you uncover beliefs that strike you as being thought viruses. If so, consider yourself fortunate to have found them. Now you can defend yourself and prevent them from spreading.

At this point in the process, you should have your problem clearly in mind, and your outcome clearly stated. In other words, your internal code should be clear and consistent in your thinking about this problem or situation. That is what you need so that you can move forward in solving it. In the next chapter you'll learn to categorize this problem as a final step in clarifying the problem space. It is also the first step in developing a solution space.

CHAPTER 5

Experience

I stressed in the last chapter that we are all products of our past experiences, or victims as the case may be. I also made the point that the world does what it always does: provides both obstacles and resources for us on the journey toward our goals. Well, our *experience* is the same in this respect. We all have within us a wealth of experience, both useful and useless, to draw from. Knowing how to tap into this is quite an art, but as always, there is a structure to the process.

Present Experience

Of course, before going into our pasts to find what we need, it's always a good idea to check to see where we are now. I find it useful at this stage to again look over some of our basic assumptions about life, as we did in Chapter 1. For example: The map is not the territory. This also means your current *experience* of the problem is not necessarily what the *problem* is, notwithstanding all of the questions you have diligently answered up to this point. A related matter here is that your past experiences are not necessarily a map to your future; the past does not have to equal the future – not at all.

Also, all behavior has some "positive" intention. People make the best choices they perceive are available to them. There are no mistakes, only outcomes. There are no failures, only feedback. In Chapter 1 you considered these ideas and to let yourself off the hook, so to speak, for whatever kind of problem, or mess, you think you may have created. Hopefully by now you have ridded yourself of the kind of negative thinking that will slow you down, or even prevent you from getting where you want to go. If not, now is the time.

Remember, too, that everyone has all of the internal resources they really need. You may not have found them yet, but you'll learn that part soon. Getting and using experiences from your past that will help you move smoothly into your future is what most of the second half of this book is about. Still, for now, it may be that you already have a set of experiences that are helping you, or hindering you, from solving your problem or making a change. Remember also, that all the information you need can be obtained through clear and open sensory channels. The cause of your difficulty, or even the solution to it, may be right in front of you, but obscured from your view by your thoughts and feelings.

What have you tried this time? In other words, what have you been doing, up to this point, to try to solve the problem, improve the situation or move toward your goal or outcome? What has happened as you tried these things?

Remember, just because something hasn't worked as you hoped it would, it doesn't necessarily mean that everything about it is wrong or ineffective. It may need more time, maybe only some slight adjustment, perhaps repetition (especially if other people are involved) - something added or something removed.

There is almost no limit to the number or kinds of problems that people can have, even when the context is narrowed down to business. It is possible, though, to organize our thinking about problem solving into categories or types of problems to be solved. If we do this on the basis of the kinds of areas of analysis we've been discussing, it can even help us in understanding how to tap into our past experiences for useful resources. I've broken down the types of problems business people generally have to deal with into five basic types, with smaller categories under each one:

1. Personal (individual) problems
      a) Creativity/Innovation
      b) Motivation
      c) Focus
      d) Planning, productivity & limitations
      e) Tools, materials, support, time/space
      f) Neuro-logical levels

2. Interpersonal/Communication problems
      a) Vision
      b) Intention
      c) Clarity, Understanding
      d) Rapport
      e) Objections

3. Training problems
    a) Training effectiveness
    b) Knowledge, Skills & Procedures
    c) Systemic effects
    d) Neuro-logical level effects

4. Systemic problems
    a) Design flaws & communication
    b) Timing & System reverberation

5. Environmental/Situational problems

Certainly these categories are not perfect and they're hardly mutually exclusive. They are simply a starting point for organizing our thinking so that we can plan for changes. Also, they will help us, when we later tap into past experiences for resources, to know which experiences are relevant and useful.

Personal (individual) problems

This does not necessarily mean that you, or someone else, has emotional or psychological problems, just that the problem is primarily confined to (or the responsibility of) one person. If this is the case, you generally know it on some level, even though it may be difficult to admit to yourself that the problem is yours. After having gone through Chapter 1, on defining who you are in this situation, you undoubtedly found that at least some part of it was related to specific beliefs, or presuppositions. Probably, you had the ability to see and understand how these can get in your way. In addition to difficulties stemming from basic beliefs and values, there are a number of other kinds of problems that basically have their focus on one individual.

a) Creativity/Innovation
Perhaps what you need is some new idea, or new way of arranging the elements of the situation, so that you can solve the problem. Creativity and the ability to innovate are often needed in difficult situations. Maybe you haven't been creative enough yet. There are a number of strategies for creativity that you may not have been exposed to before now.

Later in the book I'll show you some of them, as well as helping you get into states where you have your best creativity right at hand. So if you feel this is the root of your problem, you're in luck.

b) Motivation

Another common problem is one of motivation. Not that people don't want to solve their problems and achieve their goals, just that they haven't the drive to work through them for some reason. I don't believe this generally to be a problem of laziness (though certainly in some cases it is). More often, the experience of the problem has drained the energy right out of the person (or you) so they just want to escape with their life and some portion of their remaining sanity. We can all sympathize. We've all been there. This, again, is solved by a change of state which we'll explore later. First, though, we must recognize if this is what is actually going on.

c) Focus

A second kind of problem, certainly related to motivation, also occurs quite often. It's also related to creativity, innovation and the choice of an outcome or goal. Focus. It is one we have probably all seen or heard about at some time, without perhaps recognizing how it actually works. An example: a friend of mine is extremely creative at coming up with new ideas for businesses. Years ago, before any of us heard about such an idea, he devised the concept of a "wellness center". *Now* most of us know exactly what that means: a "holistically" oriented place where people concentrate on staying healthy and preventing illness, as opposed to getting help after they have become sick or gotten hurt (even though many of these have *devolved* back into standard medical settings in which people simply go for repair work).

The center he envisioned at the time was to combine classes on stress management and problem solving, exercise and fitness with all the latest equipment, general health and diet aids and lots of other services. He found the land on which to build it, had a beautiful set of plans drawn up by an architect, and lined up the money at the bank. Just before construction was to begin, though, he decided to expand the concept to another level of services including industrial and corporate training and development. So the architect had to draw up new plans and the construction people had to wait. When this work was complete and construction ready to begin again, another new idea popped up. How about a complete mental health facility? Something like a corner neighborhood health center, only for emotional and family problems? Well this involved a new set of drawings, including lots of office space, an additional set of people to manage and work in the setting, and lots of other details. Before this could be worked out, guess what? Yep, more good ideas. A franchise system of centers, just like this one, all over the country. Along with a computerized heart screening service. Along with after school tutoring and special education help for clients, in addition to all the other myriad services, etc. etc. etc.

As you may have guessed, the whole project ended up being scrapped. Lining up the right people, getting the plans done, all of the construction problems that were going to come up, and the sheer size of the project had become *overwhelming* to its creator. He had to walk away.

d) Planning, productivity & limitations

The important thing about this story about my friend is that the problem is two-fold. First and foremost is that the kind of thinking that goes into creativity and innovation is not the same as that which is needed for *implementation*. In fact, these two kinds of thinking can be so different that they become antagonistic to one another. Probably all of us have met someone or at least heard about some poor soul who is forever coming up with great ideas but can't carry them through to a finished product. We call them "dreamers". Many artists have problems like this. The creative side of art, music, film and literature can be totally at odds with the business side. On the other hand, we all know people, as well, who are great gung-ho workers as long as someone tells them what to do. They don't use their creativity much, but they are as motivated to do a good job as anyone. To do both of these things well is merely a matter of using the right kind of thinking and strategies, at the right time and in the right order. In this case:

Figure 5.i

Creativity ➡Motivation ➡ Implementation

Linear Creativity Model

To be successful, you have to have all of these abilities available, and they need to come in the right order, without getting in the way of each other. In a large enough company, different functional units, or departments, can actually be assigned the different roles. In smaller companies, perhaps a different individual will take on each task. For one person to do it all, however, takes the special set of abilities involved, plus the ability to do each one in the right sequence.

Remember, this problem was two-fold. The second part of the problem, which in the case of my friend was the more telling, was the value, or criteria, level of analysis. In other words, he got stuck at the question: "How will I know, when I'm done designing the center, if it's good enough?" Also, "How will I know it's the right time to get motivated and energized to build it?" Then, "How will I know, while I'm building (implementing the idea), and even after it's finished, if it was what I really intended?" "That I've accomplished my goal?" "That I'm successful?" This is not only a problem of sequence, but of personal values.

Having gone through the section on outcomes in Chapter 2, you know the importance of having well defined measures. It is also, obviously, important to be able to measure *as you go along*. This is called feedback. It involves being able to know that you are carrying out what you developed when you were in the state of creativity and innovation. To do this well means that you have to, while creating, imagine moving into the future, when you'll be implementing. That way you can predict where and when you will measure, or in some way evaluate, your effectiveness. This process is called feedforward. To expand the earlier image:

Figure 5.ii

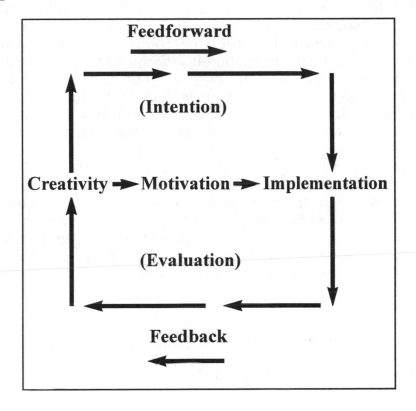

Systemic Creativity Model

This cyclical, systemic kind of thinking is extremely valuable in planning projects of any kind. My friend realized some time after walking away from his dream that he hadn't considered enough while he was in the developing stage. Mainly, his own standards. He realized that unless he could do something absolutely super, he wouldn't feel good about it. As he finished each step in the planning process he felt a bit let down. The only way he could get his good feelings back about the project was to create something new and bigger. Each of those, in turn, made the implementation that much more difficult and involved. And he had to add more people. The problem then became finding people with *his* vision, standards, dedication and the personal need to do something truly great. He ended up with too big a chunk and too little help. Each time he began to implement his idea, he would think back to the creativity stage (feedback) and see that he would have to make too many compromises. Then he would lose his motivation. So he would go back to the creative phase, where he felt the most comfortable, and expand again. As he imagined implementation (feedforward) he would realize how many more people, and how much time, he was going to need and become unclear about how to do it (much less how to measure his success). This would dampen his motivation again. The only way to get his enthusiasm back was more planning. He had no way to stop this cycle himself. Outside forces eventually stepped in and stopped it for him.

The five part model of Self, Purpose, Audience, Code and Experience is actually a project planning model originally developed for writing projects such as reports and books. If you use it, your planning and implementation of solutions to problems should go much more smoothly. Doing a thorough job in the planning stages always makes the rest of the job easier.

e) Tools, materials, support, time/space

Balancing the creativity, motivation, and *practicality* issues in any project are, of course, also necessary prerequisites to success. The idea of practicality leads us to the next category of common personal business problems: The right tools and materials, the right support, and the time and space to work effectively. Obviously some of this is dictated by forces outside of any one person. But it is up to each of us to take the responsibility to at least notice whether we have these things. If not, we must try our best to get them. Otherwise, we are *choosing* to do less than we're capable of.

f) Neuro-logical levels

Finally, again consider the neuro-logical levels of Identity, Belief, Capability, Behavior and Environment as we did in the last chapter. If you think about it, we have been talking about these as we went through this entire discussion. Think about the example. My friend really has a strong identity, and he knows himself well. During this project he had a conflict on the level of beliefs, however, because he believed that if he did less than an extraordinary job, it would reflect on *who* he was as a person–in effect, weaken his identity. He clearly had the capability to be creative, motivated and constructive. But he did not act, on the behavioral level, in a sequence that was productive. Finally, though he handled the environmental concerns well at the beginning, by the time the project had grown so large, the business environment could no longer support the project.

As a solution, when he realized all of this, he chose a somewhat smaller project that he could maintain control over without having to rely on the outside environment in the same way. Also, he enlisted the help of someone extremely good at implementation and just as dedicated to the project. This allowed him to focus on the design. Finally, he allowed for the project to grow in natural stages, without having to, in effect, finish before he started. He attributes his current success in this new project to understanding his own personal needs, goals and abilities. He's a lot happier, too.

Before answering the following questions, take another look over your answers to the ones in Chapter 1. They will help you focus on any personal or individual issues that may be part of your present problem or situation.

Questions:

1. When you are being creative or innovative, is it difficult for you? Do you have a hard time imagining carrying out your plans?
2. Can you feel comfortable with achieving your outcome, now, and believe that it is possible and worthwhile?
3. Are you able, now, to imagine achieving your outcome and goals, and see how you will measure your results at various intervals? Can you control both the feedforward of your intentions and adjust for the feedback of your evaluations and measurements?
4. Do you know when it will be time to stop this project, or to move from one phase to another?
5. Do you feel you have the support, tools & materials, time and space to reach your goals?
6. Do you think this current problem or difficulty is the result of something personal to you? Can you identify it as fitting one or more of the sub-categories we just discussed? If so, does this help you clearly understand how this problem is framed? What you need to focus on to change?

7. If, indeed, you believe you have identified the problem as falling into the above category, can you remember, now, a time when you had a similar problem? One that was of the same type, structured much the same way, that you were *able to solve* effectively?

If so, spend a few minutes thinking back through this past similar situation and remembering as much of it as you can, as vividly as you can. You might want to make some notes about similar features between that past difficulty and this current one. Save these notes for later.

Interpersonal/Communication problems

Now we come to problems that exist between two or more people. Undoubtedly the most common complaint among business people is a complaint about someone else. Communication problems abound in all areas of our lives, not just business. Fortunately, communication problems, really all problems between people, are the simplest (though not necessarily easiest) to repair.

a) Vision

The first kind is one in which two or more people have differing visions about what it is they are trying to accomplish. It's an axiom of traditional business practices that vision needs to come from the top down (though lately many of us think this can be quite short-sighted). In other words, whoever is most in charge needs to be the one deciding on what kind of business the company is in. Then that person, or board, management team or whatever needs to clearly communicate that vision to everyone else in the company, in a way they can really appreciate and *share*. It isn't enough for them just to know the vision of their leaders, they must *operate* with the same one. The Total Quality movement has taught us that vision can come from the bottom just as well as the top, but the point is that everyone shares the same vision, regardless of where it came from. In NLP terms we might say that everyone needs to be looking at the same pictures in their minds; working from the *same map*.

b) Intention

Often when someone communicates something to someone else, they can do it very clearly and well, but leave out what they *intend* by that communication. This is why you answered so many questions about your basic presuppositions at the beginning of this book.

In communication theory we have the concept of messages and *meta*-messages. The message is the one you give directly to the people you are communicating with: the words. The meta-message is the communication *about* the message that *conveys your intention*. Have you ever had someone tell you that they were really interested in what you had to say, while at the same time looking at something else, reading something on their desk, or in some way obviously not paying attention at all? Their stated message (interest) is less believable than the meta-message (they don't care). These meta-messages come in a variety of flavors from subtle body language, to failure to follow through on promises. They are at least as important as the messages that go with them but often the most difficult to interpret.

To be clear, first you must clarify these intentions and values for yourself. Then you can communicate them to others. The ideal is to have your meta-messages support your stated messages, by being *congruent* with (matching) them. If you are *incongruent* in your communication, people won't know what to believe. They'll act like it, too.

Another problem with unclear intentions or incongruent communication is that the people you give responsibility to may not know how to make decisions on their own. Many complaints about employees lacking creativity or incentive are really the fault of the people in charge. Far too often what the employees really lack is a basic understanding about why they are doing what they've been assigned in the first place. This leads to the inevitable dilemma of either operating on automatic pilot, and being stuck when anything out of the ordinary happens, or making wild guesses about what to do. *The natural tendency is to do nothing*, rather than screw up.

An interesting, and excellent, example of conveying intention quite well came when I was in graduate school working as a waiter in a New Orleans restaurant. The executive chef at this restaurant, at that time, happened to be famed Cajun chef Paul Prudhomme. In a large restaurant, especially one that is part of a series or chain of restaurants, the executive chef doesn't actually do any preparation of food. He is more of a manager, a teacher, a buyer and a marketing director, rolled (pardon the pun) into one. One day a customer sent back a dish because he didn't like it. The chef happened to be in the kitchen. He asked to see the dish, a rather unusual one that they didn't generally prepare. He took one look and immediately called all of the kitchen staff together.

The first thing Chef Paul said was: "I want you all to understand my intention in having created this dish." He then calmly and systematically explained the philosophy underlying the way the dish was supposed to be prepared, to look, smell and taste. He also described what someone who knows this particular dish would expect when ordering it. Then he demonstrated the preparation, and had the kitchen staff people examine and taste it, along with the original that had been sent back, for comparison. Then he asked the staff member who had prepared the rejected one to prepare the dish in front of him, to demonstrate that he understood what he was doing, and why. Chef Paul's handling of this situation was artful, respectful, and elegant. A far cry from the typical situation in a kitchen. He left little room for misunderstanding. And no one got hurt feelings.

c) Clarity, Understanding

Problems of communicating vision and intention are so widespread that they could legitimately be considered an epidemic. Just as widespread is the problem of communicating clearly at all. This should be something we all learn growing up, but it just isn't. Communication is clear when the person who is watching and listening understands. Understanding means that the listener ends up with the same, or nearly the same, pictures, sounds and feelings (smells and tastes) inside of them that the communicator has. How the listener responds communicates that level of understanding, or the lack of it. As I've said repeatedly, it is up to the communicator to make sure that he or she is understood. Remember from Chapter 1, Presupposition #3: The meaning of the communication is the response it elicits, regardless of the communicator's intent.

d) Rapport

This leads us to the subject of rapport, one of the most important in all communication. If you are the communicator in any situation, and you don't have sufficient rapport with your listeners, not much useful will happen. Remember also that having rapport with others does not necessarily, or only, mean that they like you. More, it means that they *trust* you, feel that you *share* things in common, and that they *understand* you. The more rapport you have with people, the easier it is for you to create the same images in their mind(s) that you have in yours. That is really what rapport means; shared thoughts, shared experiences, shared feelings.

e) Objections

Remember in Chapter 1, we looked at Presupposition #8, Corollary 1:

Resistance is a sign that:

Either

Rapport has not been effectively established or maintained;

Or

Objections have not been properly considered and addressed.

Appreciating people's objections is a necessity. Handling them well is an art. Ignoring them is a disaster. Often people complain that others just don't understand or appreciate what it is they are trying to do, and constantly fight against their brilliant ideas. This again is seldom because people are lazy. More likely, it is a problem of:

1   Sharing a common vision;
2.   Understanding the legitimacy of the basic intention behind the proposal;
3.   Communicating it clearly in a way that everyone understands;
4.   Being within a framework of good rapport.

If there are still objections, once these conditions are met, then these need to be dealt with directly.

In the medical profession it has become important for professionals to be able to explain complicated procedures to laypeople–in other words, to the rest of us. If you go into a doctor's office, or a hospital, if you're smart you ask plenty of questions. Your goal is to make sure that you are getting the best care possible. The only way to know is to get as much of the *doctor's* understanding (vision & intention), clearly in your mind (your understanding), in a relationship of trust (rapport), so that you will agree on a course of treatment (without objections). If you don't get to that point, you are absolutely justified in asking to get a second (third, fourth, ...) opinion until you are satisfied. Most of us, nowadays, feel quite justified in being demanding of professionals who have our care in their hands. We sometimes forget that anyone who has *their* care in *our* hands deserves the same respect and treatment.

If you think this area may be trouble for you, I suggest that you review your answers to those in Chapters 2 & 3, on Purpose and Audience respectively, before answering the following questions. They will help you focus on your intentions and how you have communicated these to those others who may be involved with you.

Questions:

1. Is your vision of your outcome and goals clear to you now? Have you communicated this vision accurately and adequately to others involved? How do you know if you have or have not communicated effectively?
2. Have you consistently communicated your intentions, along with instructions, suggestions and requests to others? In a way that they could appreciate and use? Congruently?
3. What evidence do you have that you have established and maintained good rapport with those around you in this situation? Have there been times when you felt that relations were strained, or needed some bolstering?
4. Have you really been hearing and appreciating any objections that others have raised to your ideas? Do you know if these are the result of lack of understanding, poor rapport or real concerns?
5. Do you think that the crux of this problem or situation is in this area of interpersonal relations and communication? Do you have good evidence for this? Does it help clarify what you need to do?

6. If you believe you have identified the problem as falling into this category of interpersonal or communication problems, can you remember a time when you had a problem or situation similar to this? One that was of the same type, structured much the same way, that you were able to solve effectively, and reach a good outcome?

    If so, spend a few minutes thinking back through this past similar situation and remembering as much of it as you can, as vividly as you can. Make some notes about similar features between that past difficulty and this current one and save them for later.

Training problems

Problems that involve, or indeed could be solved by, training cover every possible area of business practices. Of course, to cover training needs analysis, design and implementation, which is way beyond the scope of this book. However it is possible to become more keenly aware of areas that might need a training solution when you are analyzing a problem.

a) Training effectiveness

A general rule is that every type of problem we've discussed so far, that is personal and interpersonal/communication problems, can be *affected* by training. This means they can be the result of poor or non-existent training or that they could be improved or eliminated by good training. In general, the problem types that follow, systemic and environmental/situational, are less able to be influenced by training. This makes sense if you think about it. The first two categories are people oriented, the last two are design, or structure, oriented. Certainly good training can help people design, or redesign a structure, but that, again, usually involves changes on the personal and interpersonal levels.

CHANGE MANAGEMENT

Managing change is a difficult thing for some people in their own lives, and therefore even harder in organizations. Much of our focus is on change in organizations, as it relates to solving specific problems. I've found that some basic principles of change have been helpful for people in focusing on implementing solutions. Here are 10 important things to remember about instituting change in an organization.

1. There will be changes.
2. Change is natural, especially in the development of any system.
3. Some people will resist change simply because it is change. They have learned that change is difficult and/or dangerous and they are simply trying to protect themselves. It isn't bad or wrong, it's necessary to recognize.
4. People and organizations that manage change well will thrive; those that don't will fail.
5. As we've said, people need three things to be willing to make change:
    Motivation–why the change is important
    Means–how the change can be accomplished
    Opportunity–the chance to make it work and to do their best
6. They also need to perceive that they are safe during and after the change.
7. All changes that are made need to be communicated clearly to everyone involved (in the case of small and interconnected organizations, that means everyone).
8. The results of changes need to be measured, reviewed and discussed at some logical interval after the change is implemented to see if the desired results have been achieved–probably at several intervals.
9. Everyone needs to feel a part of every change, and that they are at least listened to. People can accept changes, even those they don't want, a lot more easily if they get to say their piece, express doubts and concerns, and (sometimes) moan and groan-even when the decision is beyond their control or authority.
10. Change is healthy and natural. Stagnation is death.

b) Knowledge, Skills & Procedures

One way to analyze a training need is to go back over the first two problem types that we have covered and pin-point the source of the problem. Then ask yourself, or anyone else involved what kind of specific knowledge, skills or procedures could be taught or trained that would alleviate the cause (remembering to keep the difference between knowledge or ability and *motivation* clearly in mind). Training needs to be designed with very specific goals in mind.

Each task that a person has to do to be effective in his or her job is a trainable task. First these have to be determined. This is usually accomplished through a process called task-analysis (just like it sounds). Then the specific skills that make up that task need to be identified and a training design built that will insure that the participants in the class or training group learn and are able to perform the skills. Then it has to be delivered, and the results measured. This process involves a great deal of cause-effect thinking; quite useful in determining training needs.

c) Systemic effects

You also need to look at the entire structure of the organization to determine how it will be affected by any change in knowledge, skills or procedures in the people to be trained. Not only do you need to analyze causes and effects in individual jobs and tasks, but also how these activities force the people involved to interact with other people, and their jobs and tasks. Also, what effects are produced in the final production of your product or service. Systemic thinking (holistic) is not the same as cause-effect thinking (lincar). They support one another.

d) Neuro-logical level effects

This is another area in which the neuro-logical levels can help in sort of a diagnostic way. Most training takes place on, and is designed to affect, the behavioral and capability levels of analysis. But when you do that, you certainly have to consider the environment in which the behaviors and capabilities are built.

Beyond those levels, it is important to remember that training always affects beliefs and identity. When you tell someone they need training, they may ask themselves questions about their value as an employee, and how you think about them. There will be a meta-message. You should be clear about what it is or you could run into real trouble implementing your training. Some people can see a suggestion for more training as an insult, some as a reward, even a statement of their importance.

The meta-messages given to people about the training they are assigned can set the whole tone that they take with them into the classroom. Years ago I participated in some research and consulting for the U.S. Army Recruiting Command. During this project we found out how the Army dealt with recruiters who were having a difficult time and needed more training. They were placed in the "I.R.P.": Ineffective Recruiters Program. Every recruiter I met knew, *intellectually*, that the program was a good one, and really was intended to help them if they were having trouble. However, the thought of being slapped with that "Ineffective" label canceled out a lot of the program's value. Bad meta-message. If the people who designed it, and came up with the name, had considered the belief and identity levels they would *never* have called it that. The label made it hard on everyone. Most trainers will tell you that the toughest experience they can face is to walk into a roomful of people who don't want to be there.

The Quality (TQM, CQI, etc.) movement in this country is designed to instill worthwhile meta-messages into communication. Training is a key factor in this, and its goal is to "insure quality" (worthwhile meta-message), not "correct bad behavior" (punitive meta-message). The other important part of Quality, in this sense, is that communication is expected, and accepted, from the bottom to the top in the organization, as I mentioned earlier. This "bottom-up" communication design also sends a meta-message that the people at the bottom, and their opinions, are valued. Sometimes asking people what kind of training they think they need can get very candid and useful answers and ideas.

Again, many of these issues of training analysis, design and delivery are beyond the scope of this book. Still, keeping these basic concepts in mind is worthwhile.

Questions:

1. Have you identified specific areas, either personally or interpersonally, that you believe could be affected or benefited by a training intervention?
2. If you believe this problem or situation could be improved by further training, can you state, very specifically what, and who, should be taught?
3. How would the people who need this training feel about it? How could you approach them in a useful, supportive and understanding way? What meta-message would you like to convey?
4. If you were to implement specific training programs to make changes in the behavior of yourself or others, do you know what kind of effects this would have on the system as a whole? How about on other areas or parts of the system, or other people besides those in the training?
5. If you were to implement a training program of some sort, could you think through, now, all of the neuro-logical levels of analysis to *plan* for the training to be a positive and useful experience for everyone? What should they do after the training, what should they be capable of, what should they believe? Who else should be involved in thinking this through?
6. Do you believe that the solution to your problems could indeed lie in training? Do you remember some past experience that seems to have the same features as this one, in which training provided a useful solution and led to a positive outcome?

   If so, spend some time thinking back through this past similar situation, remembering as much of it as you can, as vividly as you can. Make some notes about similar features and save them for later.

Systemic problems

Some people in business have studied systems design and analysis, but the vast majority haven't. As with some of the other topics here, there is no way to do justice to such a broad subject (and there are a number of good books on "learning organizations" and "re-engineering" that do). It isn't really necessary in order to help you solve your problems or make changes. But, thinking about some of the most common ways that people run into systemic, or structural, problems can help you in determining what to do about them.

a) Design flaws & communication

The broadest sub-category here, undoubtedly, is basic design flaws in the system. Some things just don't work no matter how hard you try to make them. Occasionally these problems are plainly obvious. For example, there may actually be some necessary component missing to effectively produce and deliver a product or service. These tend to be so obvious, though, that they are readily repaired (if they were problems too long, you wouldn't be in business). More often these problems show up in personal or interpersonal ways. People find that they aren't communicating, that "the right hand and the left hand" don't know what the other is doing. Obviously, this can happen for a lot of reasons. Sometimes, it's built into the system.

Recently I heard of a case in which some administrators made the decision to *forbid* communication between different divisions of a company (a *really lousy* meta-message). Their stated intention was to work with, motivate and measure the success of each division, independently, avoiding unproductive competition. They *really* believed this would give them greater control over operations. The actual effect, however, was to isolate each division to the point where everyone in the divisions felt that they had been "cut loose" by management, without support. Morale and productivity sunk into the pits. What eventually happened was that the "informal" communication system, the one nobody in management could control, took over. People from different divisions ran into each other outside of work, or called each other in secret. They shared experiences and problems with one another; discovering that they were being told different stories by management about the state of the business and the successes and failures of the other divisions. Then they *revolted*. The upshot was that management was forced to bring everyone together to solve the problem they had created. Though morale quickly turned around, the cost in trust and hurt feelings was much higher than it needed to be.

It is always important to remember that no structure is totally controlled by anyone. People in hospitals often point out that it is mainly the nurses who run the show, not the doctors and administrators. That's because they are the ones delivering most of the service, and information, directly to the patients (customers). In many large offices, the clerical staff runs things. That's because they too control the lines of communication. Some people who have worked in academic systems, such as universities, or the public sector, have pointed out that it often seems like no one is in control ...

The point is that people have to communicate with one another to do their jobs. The larger the organization, the more complicated the lines of communication. This makes for more chances for mis-communication and also, more likely that people will develop their own means of getting things done, without using the organization, or its rules. People will *work the system*, when it's the only way to work.

The clearest example is the former Soviet Union. The bureaucracy had become so unwieldy that an entire "off-the-books" economy (black market) had developed to feed and clothe people. Then Gorbachev and others tried to reform the system of government. Though they were well-intentioned, they were unable to control *the informal system* that was actually providing a large percentage of goods and services. Eventually, the Soviet Union began to break up into pieces, along historical and ethnic lines, with a thriving black market economy and an astonishing organized crime network.

It must be clearly said that people don't have to develop these strategies to go around authority, when authority works *effectively*. They always do it *in response to a perceived need*. Good authority stays abreast of, and on top of, what is needed so that it can provide solutions effectively. Otherwise, the informal methods will develop. Responsiveness is the key.

b) Timing & System reverberation

Another factor in dealing with systems is one of timing. The time it takes a system, or company, to design, develop and deliver a product is obviously crucial to success. This time is built into, and governed by, the structure of the system. How long communication takes from one part to another, and back around again, can mean the difference between innovation and defeat.

There is a principal known as *system reverberation* that needs to be addressed here because very few people are aware of it at all. If you throw a bottle into the ocean with a message in it, it may bring you a rescuer in time. But you wouldn't expect it to be very soon. By the same token, if you make a change in an organization (feedforward), it takes time for the results to go all the way through the system and back to you (feedback). For example, if you send out a memo about a new policy, it may have to go through some channels. Then it must get to each person affected by it. Then each one of them must interpret it, and follow the new procedure. Then the system has to produce its result. How long does all this take? Well, of course, there is no one answer for that. It depends on:

1. The *size* of the organization
2. The number of people *involved*
3. The number of people *affected*, and
4. How long it takes to *notice* the result.

This means that you have to be patient enough to wait for a change. It also means you have to be *expecting* it when it comes back to you. Finally, and often most importantly, you must *interpret* the results in relationship to what you sent out in the first place.

This phenomenon of system reverberation turns out to cause many more problems than people are generally aware of. The reason is that it is easy to continually send out new messages through the system or organization, without waiting for the previous messages to cycle back through. This makes it difficult, or impossible, to know which messages cause (or prevent) changes. It's an easy trap to fall into unless you have *patience*.

The same can be said of issues of personnel, and especially training. Many people expect those who work with, or for, them to immediately know how to do their jobs as they are designed to be done. But learning takes time: "the learning curve". Also, the results of training often spread out over time, so that even if someone is doing a really good job, the results of that job may not be noticeable right away. It takes time to know if a problem can be solved by training. Many problems can, but it takes care, skill and attention to detail to make training work. A good tip for managers is to think of training like any other *capital investment*, amortized over time, rather than a quick fix with a quick return.

Questions:

1. Have you considered structural flaws in your organization as the cause of your current difficulties? Do you have some evidence that this might be the case? Do you understand how they operate?
2. Who do you believe is in control of your company or organization? How is this control exercised? How do you know?
3. Are you aware of an informal communication, or operations, system within your more formal structure? How does it work? Is it useful, or harmful? Who controls it?
4. How do the lines of communication in your company really work? How long does it take to get things done? How long does it take to see, hear or feel the results of changes that are implemented? How does the feedback come back to you? To others?
5. Do you believe that the source of your problem is something in the way the system works? Do you have some specific evidence for this, or some way to adequately test it?

   If this is the case, can you remember some past experience that seems to have the same features as this one, in which you were able to arrive at a useful solution that led to a positive outcome?

   If so, spend some time thinking back through this past similar situation and remembering as much of it as you can, as vividly as you can. Make some notes about similar features, especially ideas about how the structure and lines of communication really work. Save them for later.

Environmental/Situational problems

It is seldom possible to change the outside environment in which we operate our businesses, though there are certainly exceptions. Usually, if we are undergoing pressure from the outside, we need to change something on the inside in response. That's the part we have control over. We may not be able to improve the overall economy we operate in, but we can certainly change the way we do business to adjust for it.

Inevitably, the changes we can make will fall into the categories of problems we have already discussed. That isn't to say that we need to label the problem differently, just change our focus to what we can do. There are a number of wise thinkers who would say that there are never any problems that can legitimately be blamed on outside forces. They point out that *someone* is always making a profit, and achieving success, no matter how bad things get. They also generally say that it doesn't matter where you think these problems come from because the result is going to be the same no matter what: You will make necessary changes and move toward your goals, or you won't. The responsibility is yours.

Questions:

1. Have you exhausted all of the other categories as the source of your present problem or difficulties? Are you sure that none of them really applies?
2. If you are convinced that the problems you are having are the result of outside forces, what specific evidence do you have to support this? Have, or would, others agree that the root of the problem is *outside* your organization?
3. Is it possible to affect the outside environment or situation directly? Safely?
4. What internal changes could you make that would change the way your system operates, and interacts, with those outside forces? Is it possible to affect the outside environment or situation directly?
5. Can you remember some past experience that seems to have the same features as this one, in which you were able to arrive at a useful solution that led to a positive outcome?
   If so, spend some time thinking back through this past similar situation and remembering as much of it as you can, as vividly as you can. Make some notes about similar features, especially regarding dealing with outside structures, and save them for later.

Past Experience & Problem Types

The value to identifying, or narrowing down, the type of problem you have to a specific category is that it narrows down your search for solutions. It also narrows down the kind of states you might want to use to develop new solutions, based on your past experiences. The remainder of this book is devoted to systematically showing you how to do just that. If you have already remembered some past similar problems, and made some good notes about them, it will help. If not, don't worry. I'll guide you further in that process.

You may, in fact, have already solved your problem by remembering how you solved a similar one in the past. Even so, you may have some difficulty in the future in which you'll need to do more. The idea, here, is not just to find solutions by comparing present problems with past ones. That is only one possibility. What I intend to show you in the second half of the book will teach you about states of consciousness and how we can use specific ones to take us all the way to our goals. It is the *way of thinking* that you will learn from; much more than the actual solutions you've used before.

Part 1

Defining Your Problem SPACE

Underview

The task up to this point in this book has been to clearly define the Problem SPACE. This means having an understanding of the actual structure of the problem or situation you wish to make a change in. Obviously if the problem involved more people than you had originally considered, and you have now included these other people, the problem space is larger. It is also, because it is more appropriate, more likely that you can effectively make the change that you want. By the same token, if the problem was really the result of your thinking about it, and not the actions of others, the problem space may actually be smaller. If this is the case, and you have recognized it, you also have a much greater chance of developing a workable solution. Certainly the right, or at least most appropriate for who you are, goals and outcomes are important as well. A well-formed outcome, and a new internal code for thinking about what it is that you want, may have changed the "shape" of the problem space. All of the questions you've answered were meant to expand or contract your image of the problem situation to the appropriate size and shape. Adding in this scheme of categorizing the problems into types should also narrow down your focus so that you can begin to develop solutions. You may have already.

PART II

PART II

Using States of Consciousness

Overview

Once you've defined your Problem SPACE, it's time to go about the task of developing solutions. As I've implied already, there is no wrong way to go about finding solutions to problems. Some ways are more thorough than others, and therefore more likely to insure success.

In this second half of the book, we will explore how to use your states of consciousness for a variety of purposes including creativity, motivation, clarity, focus and more. We will also apply particular states to particular problem types, as we defined them in Chapter 5.

This part of the book is highly systematic. It contains a number of experiments, highly structured and carefully ordered to accomplish our tasks. One of these tasks is to make using states, and the technology of NLP, a regular and natural part of your ongoing behavior. Another is to get directly to a solution that will work for your current problem or situation, and get you to your intended well formed outcome.

It is important that you go through the experiments carefully, and in order. Otherwise you may get confused, or find that you have gone off on a tangent away from the direction of your desired outcome. Even though some of the experiments may seem repetitive or unnecessary, they should be done anyway. You'll be thankful later. During the process you will undoubt-edly learn more about your thinking processes than you ever have before. It's your reward for being diligent. Enjoy!

CHAPTER 6

Understanding States

States

What are states of consciousness? A number of terms immediately come to mind that mean roughly the same thing. Frame of mind, state of awareness, mood and terms like those are all pretty close. Generally, when people talk about the subject in useful terms, though, they are talking about particular states, with particular characteristics. We might mean the right state of mind for working, or for getting organized, or for being creative, or creatively solving problems. These can be specific states. The important thing for our purposes here is that we have a method for:

1. Distinguishing one state from another;
2. So that we can explore its usefulness;
3. Modify or enhance it;
4. Control it and get it back whenever we want it.

States are individual and personal. So it is usually best to talk about the *experience* of being in a particular state. We all go in and out of many states of consciousness all the time. Probably hundreds each day. These are what are called *natural* states; not the most useful term. Neither is the term *altered* state since we aren't really sure what is altered, for whom, when, where or why. Some states are clearly easier to tell from others, however.

Sleep is easy to tell from wakefulness. But sleep and wakefulness are not really discrete individual states. Each contains many possible states or levels of consciousness. For example, deep sleep differs markedly from dream or REM (rapid eye movement) sleep. Hypnotic states differ from both sleep and wakefulness and also include many varieties. Even hypnosis does not produce a *particular* discrete state. Rather it is a tool for going from one state to another. Like any tool, it has many uses and many results. The tool can't decide whether the state we get to is worthwhile or not. We have to make that decision.

This brings us to the method for identifying particular discrete states. Since we are going to do so in terms of experience and behavior, first we need to find a way of talking about states. In other words, our descriptions of complicated events and conditions have to be plain enough so that we all know what we're talking about.

Sensory Experience

In NLP we have a notation we use to distinguish a particular state of consciousness. It is called the 4-tuple, meaning that it is a unit made up of four parts, based on the five senses. The four parts are:

V - Visual	(Sight)
A - Auditory	(Sound)
K - Kinesthetic	(Feeling)
O-G - Olfactory-Gustatory	(Smell-Taste)

It turns out that we not only take in information through our five senses, but we also store and process it that way in our minds, and in fact communicate it that way through language. So the five senses are involved in the three major information processes of input, internal processing and output.

Figure 6

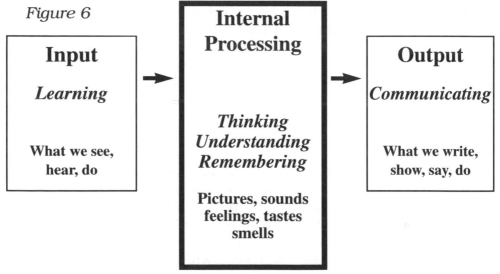

Information Processing

For our purposes, the internal processing is what we will concentrate on. In the 4-tuple, then, visual refers to our internal pictures, auditory to internal sounds, kinesthetic to feelings, olfactory-gustatory, which we combine for convenience, to smells and tastes. A particular state of consciousness, is the combination of these four components (a 4-tuple), inside our minds at any moment in time.

Remember this is only an *experiential* definition of a state of consciousness. It doesn't include any *physiological* data (such as blood pressure, heart rate, temperature, respiration, blood sugar level, pupil dilation, galvanic skin response, etc.) because that isn't important for our purposes. Rest assured that these physiological variables *do change* as the internal components of our experience change (which you can verify if you use the NeuroLink). In fact, the physiological component is what makes all of this work.

To start with, we need a convenient way of distinguishing between different states; a way that we can verify by ourselves, that is specific. Just as in defining our outcomes and goals, this is easiest in sensory terms. We cannot always know when we have changed physiologically (unless we use the NeuroLink) but we *can* know when we have changed something in our experience. We'll see, hear or feel it.

States work like systems. When one part of a state has changed, it will have a ripple effect on the other parts. That is how we go from one state to another. We can control the pictures in our minds, what we say to ourselves, and so forth. So we can choose, at will, to change a state we don't like to one we do. Then we can use that particular state to accomplish a particular purpose, whenever we need to.

To begin with, we can think of each of the sensory modalities (vision, hearing, feeling) as an independent part. Often, we are only aware of our internal visualizations, the pictures in our minds, and not much else. The same can be said of our feelings or any of the other senses. Changing what we pay attention to, from one sense to another for example, can alter our total experience.

Another way to change our experience of something (alter our state) is to change the *content* of our internal images of what is going on. This will change our feelings about it, provided we pick the *right* changes. For example, a common exercise given to performers to overcome stage fright, is to imagine the audience sitting in their underwear (or some other stupid position). For ourselves, we could imagine what someone would look and sound like, after mis-treating us in some way, if they were apologizing profusely, or admitting they were foolish and wrong. It is difficult to be frightened by people who are in a more vulnerable (or ridiculous) position than we are. We have all played games of this sort in the privacy of our own thoughts at some time or other. We just don't usually do it *systematically*, whenever it would help us. But we could.

Sub-Modalities

There is another, more powerful way to change our experience, besides changing the content of our thoughts. We can change the *form*. This is called changing *sub*-modalities. Within each sensory modality, there are a number of *characteristics* that make up the form of that modality. That is why they are called *sub*-modalities. For example, one of the sub-modalities of the visual modality (internal pictures) is *brightness*. Another is *size*. Another is *color*. Each of these can be changed without really making a new image. But the form or *quality* of the image will certainly be different. This difference will make another difference in some other part of our experience–change one part and others will follow. For example making a particular picture we have in our minds brighter, larger or clearer may make us feel differently when we think about it. It may also change the sounds we hear along with it, what we say to ourselves about it, or any number of other things. In a sense then, this makes changing sub-modalities the easiest way to control your state. The right sub-modality change can instantly change an entire experience–even something *physical*.

Visual Sub-Modalities

Think about TV. We have all used one at some time (for some of us, most of the time). As the technology has improved over the years, we have had more and more control over the picture and sound quality of our sets. Now some of them have stereo or surround sound, huge screens, remarkable resolution and color, cable or satellite hookups to make the picture and sound crystal clear. We have VCR's, or laser disc players, so we can repeat something as often as we like, skip parts we don't like, watch in slow motion, fast motion, frame by frame or even backwards. Have you ever wondered what it would be like to exercise this same kind of control over the pictures and sounds in our minds? What kind of changes could that make in our ability to think clearly and solve problems? The following experiment will give you a good start in learning how to control your internal images, and therefore your state. Let's begin by discovering what a state of excitement and enthusiasm looks and feels like for you.

EXPERIMENT: ADJUSTING VISUAL IMAGES & FEELINGS

Step 1:

Remember an event in your life in which you were extremely *excited* and *enthusiastic* about what you were doing. Imagine this as if you were back in time, having that experience over again right now. Just remembering it won't have as powerful an effect, so really *be there again*, *re-living* the experience. Whenever I ask you to re-experience something, this is what I mean.

As you think of this, pay attention to the visual image of this time that you have in your mind's eye. It could be any sort of picture, the brain is a flexible organ. Let's, for purposes of discussion, talk about it as if it is a particular scene from your memory of this event you've chosen.

Step 2:

Notice if there is motion, like a movie, or if it is frozen, like a still shot or a slide. Hold it steady in your minds eye. Notice the qualities of this picture, the size, color, brightness, whether it has a frame around it, and anything unusual that strikes you.

Step 3:

Pay close attention to the physical feelings you have in your body. Also whatever emotion you would label this. Pay special attention to just how *intense* these feelings are.

Step 4:
Now imagine that you have a brightness control knob next to the image in your mind's eye, just like the one on a television set. Imagine turning up the brightness knob, slowly, and watch the image get brighter as it would on a real TV. Make the image noticeably brighter, but still clearly the same image. Don't let it get so bright that it begins to get hazy or break up.

Step 5:
Now pay attention to the feeling that goes along with that internal image. Has it changed in any way now that the image is brighter? In what way?

Step 6:
Now turn the brightness of the picture back down, and continue to turn it down so that the image in your mind becomes dim; dim, but still barely visible as the same image.

Step 7:
Again pay attention to the feelings you have as the picture is significantly dimmed in your imagination. What changes did you notice this time?

Step 8:
Finish by bringing the brightness back to its original level.

Most people experience the intensity of their *feelings* change along with these changes in the *brightness* of the images. Usually, the brighter the image, the more intense the feelings and vice versa. This was probably what happened for you, since it is for most people. Not everyone experiences this though. Let's try with some different sub-modalities and find out what happens.

Step 1:
Retrieve the same image that you were just viewing in your mind while you adjusted the brightness.

Step 2:

This time instead of adjusting the brightness, bring the image closer to you. As close as you can while still holding the picture steady in your mind.

Step 3:

Again pay attention to any changes this causes in your feelings.

Step 4:

Now move it back away from you, even farther than it was originally. In fact, move it as far away as you can, but make sure you are still able to see it clearly.

Step 5:

How does it feel now as you look at this distant image?

Again, most people feel the feelings that go with the image actually intensify as the picture gets closer. Conversely, the feelings usually diminish as the image moves farther away. I must again stress that I'm only talking about averages now. Not everyone responds in the same way, so that's why we have to experiment for ourselves to find which of these has the most effect for us. Exactly the same experiment can be performed using any of the visual sub-modalities.

What happens if you change the size of the image in your mind? Imagine it has gone, say from a 2" screen to a 52" inch screen, proportional to its original size. Then try the reverse. Make it very small compared to its original size. The chances are that your feelings intensify as the image gets larger, and diminish as it gets smaller. Do it once more, but with color. First make the colors extremely distinct and vivid–more than the original if possible. Then try the reverse: change the picture all the way to black and white and shades of gray. Do your feelings change when you make these changes in the picture in your mind's eye? How do they compare with the changes in your feelings that came with changing brightness, distance and size? Make sure you return the images to their original form.

I know that this kind of thought experiment can seem a little strange to you. If it's your first time experimenting with your own inner thoughts and feelings, it can also be a little surprising. That is one of the reasons I want to take you through the process carefully, step by step.

Were you surprised about the effect of simply changing the brightness of an image? Think for a moment about the words "bright" and "dim" and how we use them. We have many idioms and phrases in our language that include those words, but don't seem to be related to visual imagery at all. For example, we have all heard someone talk about a "bright future". We have also heard about a "dim past". Have you ever heard people say they remembered their "bright distant past?" Or that they were "looking forward to a dim future?" Not likely. The same goes for size and color. People talk about experiences, or even other people as being "colorful" or "larger than life" when they make a special impression. By the same token people talk about things, or others, being dull or small when they make less of an impact. Most of us would like some "distance from" our problems, especially if they seem to be hovering over us precariously. Now, after doing this experiment, you know why we say these things the way we do.

Language reflects our experience. Experience begins with the senses and internal processing of information. Some linguists will argue that our most basic use of language is derived from our *feelings* about particular experiences. Those feelings are, obviously, affected by other senses. Language reflects these relationships much more than most people realize. Listening to people talk can be a real eye-opener (or ear-opener) into their internal thoughts, and senses. The same goes for reading and writing.

The point to this is that changing one sub-modality can have a powerful effect on another sub-modality, even in another sense. For example, increase the brightness of the picture in your mind, and it can increase the intensity of the feelings. These are changes in both quality and quantity. They are also totally within our control. It should be obvious that even this subtle change of one visual sub-modality can have far reaching effects on your experience. Just this one change can help you change your feelings about anything, provided that you experiment with it and make adjustments to suit your needs. Here is a list of the major visual sub-modalities followed by a brief description of each and how you can change them.

Visual Sub-Modalities

Brightness	Focus
Distance	Slide
Size	Motion Picture
Shape	Movement/Speed
Location	Associated
Direction	Disassociated
Contrast	Depth 3D/Flat
Clarity	Frame/No Frame
Color	Other?

Brightness we have already covered. It is just the same as on a TV set, how bright the picture itself actually is. In some cases this may vary inside of an image. **Contrast** also means the same as it would on a TV. Some people think of this as *sharpness*. **Clarity** is similar, but is likely to vary within an image itself, some parts being clearer than others. The same goes for **focus**. Some people have trouble distinguishing clarity and focus as separate qualities so it might help to think of them as a photographer might–a picture can be in focus, but not clear, or very sharp but with some parts not in focus. Most difficulties understanding these kinds of differences are examples of the limitations of how we use our language (not the limitations in our experience).

Color means the one(s) you see. Is the picture black and white, full color, or a combination? Does some color or colors stand out as central or important somehow?

Shape means shape of the image itself as well as internal shapes that stand out in the picture. The same goes for **size**, **distance**, and **location**. For example, the image in your mind may be a 2 foot x 3 foot rectangle, about six feet away, directly in front of you, as opposed to a one foot across circle, 18 inches away from your face.

Whether you see an internal image as a still shot, like a **slide** or photograph, or as a **motion picture**, can be crucial. So can the **depth** perception of the image: it could be flat and two-dimensional like a photo, or appear to be three-dimensional like a slide or, more dramatically, a hologram. If it is a motion picture, the **speed** and **direction** of motion(s) could be important. For example, the motion may be exactly as you remember it, if it is a memory, or it could be in slow motion. More unusual, it could be going backwards (very useful in some circumstances–you might try this with an internal movie of a very unpleasant memory and find out what happens). Sometimes you actually see an image in your mind in some other direction than directly in front (perhaps up and to your left). Another possibility is that the direction of the image, or the motion in it, has changed in some other way.

Sometimes we see a visual image in our mind's eye as if it had a **frame** around it. Sometimes it just stops at some edge, but has no frame, or line of any kind, around it. Other times images are **panoramic**, surrounding us like we were inside of them.

Last and perhaps most dramatic is **association**. An associated image is one in which you see exactly what you would see, through your own eyes, if you were there (usually a panoramic view). In other words, you would not see yourself in the image, just as you do not really see yourself now. A **disassociated** image is just the opposite. You would see yourself in the image as if you were looking through someone else's eyes. To understand better, imagine for a moment that you are in a room with a group of people and you are being videotaped. What you see while you are in the room is an associated image. The playback that you see later from the tape is disassociated, since you see yourself from another point of view, that of the camera. Do you have a more literal idea of what people are telling you when they say they need a different *perspective*, or a new point of view? They might be talking about changing from associated to disassociated images in their mind. This can be a most dramatic, and useful change. We'll come back to it later.

Auditory Sub-Modalities

Remember also, that changing sub-modalities works with all of the senses, not just internal visual images. We began with changing a visual sub-modality only because this is easiest for most people at first (The United States may be the most highly visually oriented in the world). Internal auditory (sound) changes can be just as dramatic as visual ones. You simply need to find out which changes will work best for you. Here is a good start.

EXPERIMENT: ADJUSTING INTERNAL SOUNDS & FEELINGS

Step 1:
Again remember an exciting experience you had in the past. It could be any kind of event or situation, as long as there is a feeling of excitement and energy attached to it. As I said earlier, it is important to imagine this as if you were back in time, *having* that experience over again now. This time though, make sure that it is a memory that involves other people.

In fact, it will help if you can remember a particular discussion, or people's voices or other distinct sounds that were a part of this situation. Perhaps there is a person whose voice really fired you up when you last heard it. This could be someone you like, or deeply respect in some way. It doesn't matter what the situation. The important thing is that you felt something strong during this event, and you still feel that same feeling when you remember it now. For some people it helps to remember the particular visual image that went along with this situation, and perhaps even the feelings–then the voices and sounds.

Step 2:
Make sure that you can clearly hear the voices, possibly including yours and the other person's, in your mind. Pay special attention to the *quality* of the voices, as well as the words being spoken. Are they high or low in pitch? Are they loud or soft? What direction do you hear them coming from? Are they raspy, throaty, nasal or clear. Is there a particular rhythm? Make sure you really know what they sound like as you listen to them in your mind.

Step 3:
Now pay close attention to your feelings. Make sure the feelings that go along with these voices are as definite as the feelings in the last experiment.

Step 4:
Once you know how you feel when you hear this internally, change the volume. Make the discussion seem louder in your mind than it actually was at the time it happened.

Step 5:

How do you feel now? Pay attention to any changes you experience in the intensity or quality of your feelings as the voices sound louder.

Step 6:

Now reverse the volume so that it gets, in your mind, even softer than it was originally. Feel the difference.

Step 7:

If there is a conversation between you and someone else, turn up the volume of the other person's voice while yours remains the same, or even gets softer. Then reverse it so yours is louder and the other person's voice gets softer. What happens inside as you imagine these changes? Do your feelings change when the voices do?

For almost everyone, this is a powerful indication of how we affect our feelings with the sounds in our minds. This means all of the sounds, not just voices. You can adjust the volume of anything in your mind, like music, telephones, clocks ticking, school bells, car engines, sirens, roaring crowds, thunder, the wind and rain and many others. We all have these sounds stored in our memories. They become part of important experiences for us, just like visual images and voices.

Certainly other qualities, sub-modalities, of sound can be as important as volume. Especially with voices. The tonality of a person's voice, technically called *timbre*, can be more impactful to us than just about anything else. For a quick experiment, imagine someone whose voice makes you feel frightened or intimidated. Listen carefully to the sound of their voice in your mind and check your feelings (it may help to close your eyes for a moment to fully experience this). Next, without changing the words, volume, direction or anything else, give it the tempo and tonal quality of that famous film star: *Donald Duck*! Do you find yourself chuckling at their voice now?

It's difficult to feel afraid or in awe of someone who sounds like a silly cartoon. This makes common sense. Even with the voice saying exactly what it said the first time, you can't take it too seriously. It's only logical that the quality of the *entire experience* of hearing this voice should be different, even though it's the form (sound quality) that you changed, not the content (words). Alter the voice, alter the feeling, alter the state. Getting the idea? Here is a list, and explanation, of the most important auditory sub-modalities.

Auditory Sub-Modalities

Sounds	Timbre
Words	Internal
Location	External
Pitch	Direction
Tone	Tempo
Voice (Who?)	Volume
Distance	Duration
Rhythm	Other?

The first distinction to make is whether you hear **sounds**, **words**, or both in your mind. At different times, of course we can hear as wide a variety of sounds **internally** as we can **externally**. That is another distinction to be made, whether the sound seems to be coming from inside your head or whether it seems like it is coming from somewhere on the outside. This becomes especially important when we listen to an internal **voice**. Some of us seem to hear voices as if they were coming from outside of our own heads. Not that we're hallucinating–we know the difference–but sometimes the sound seems to be located outside of us. **Whose voice** is it? Sometimes we won't recognize the voice, but it may still be clearly male or female, old or young, or have some other characteristic. Remember that paying close attention to all of these distinctions will help us recognize, reproduce, or change the sounds.

Whether the sounds seem to be coming from inside or outside, the precise **location** can be important. Then, of course, the **direction** from which the sound is coming, as well as the apparent **distance** away from us, can usually be determined. The **volume** can be a function of the distance and direction as well. Sounds usually seem softer the farther away they are, and louder as they get closer.

Also important are other qualities of sound. Thinking of musical sounds can help make these distinctions clear. One characteristic is **pitch**: how high or low the notes would be

121

on, say, a piano. If the sounds are musical there may also be a **rhythm** (beat) and **tempo** (speed). **Duration**, or how long the sound actually lasts, can be important in some instances.

Tone and **timbre** refer to frequency ranges and distributions. Without getting too technical, think of different brass instruments such as a trumpet and a saxophone. Even while playing the same note at the same volume they sound different from one another. They each have a distinctive tone and timbre. These qualities also allow us to identify a characteristic voice as distinct from others.

The reason for including all of these elements is only to remind you of the different possibilities. As you practice you will automatically consider those most important for you. Some will clearly affect your feelings more than others.

Kinesthetic Sub-Modalities

The key here is in finding the right sub-modality to change, for you, in a particular situation. You have a great many choices. What you will find is that when you have determined how a particular sub-modality change affects you, you will have a new tool for changing your experience. That sub-modality change will work the same way for you each time you use it. For example, if you find that *brightening* a particular visual image *increases the intensity of the feelings* attached to that image, it will undoubtedly work for all your internal visual images the same way. It will make the feelings more intense. That is why I suggested that you pick an image that gives you a good feeling to experiment with first. Remember that your brain will make the feelings more intense when you make the pictures brighter. It won't decide on an *unconscious* level whether or not *it's a good idea*, in each and every case. It will simply follow instructions. A feeling of pain will get more intense just like a feeling of pleasure. Be aware. To help out, here is a list of kinesthetic, or feeling, sub-modalities with some comments. This will help you pay more attention, closely and distinctly, to your feelings (not a bad idea, all by itself).

Kinesthetic Sub-Modalities

Internal	Proprioceptive
External	Shape
Location	Temperature
Weight	Movement
Duration	Intensity
Size	Moisture
Pressure	Texture
Frequency	Rhythm
Tactile	Balance
Emotion?	Other?

Again, the first thing you will probably want to consider in kinesthetics, or feelings, is whether they are on the **inside** or the **outside**. **Tactile** means the feeling of touch as opposed to **proprioception**, which means internal feelings. These include the internal sensations of body position, muscle tension, and more. Next the **intensity**, or strength of a feeling, is something we are usually quite aware of. It is also usually what we want to control.

Location is important since we can feel some things in very specific areas of our body or on our skin. Some feelings also seem to have **size** and **shape** to them. **Moisture** is certainly something we can feel on our skin, though it's usually related to temperature changes. Besides our skin, our mouths can certainly feel wet or dry, especially during certain emotions or around food.

Generally when we notice our feelings we can sense **weight**, **pressure**, and **temperature** changes, either inside of us, or on our skin. We can also feel **texture** on our skin, and some people find this to be something they always notice.

Some feelings also seem to have **movement** to them. Then we can usually distinguish the qualities of **duration** (how long), **frequency** (how often), and **rhythm** (what pattern) as well. This is especially true of natural functions such as breathing and heart rate. For some people the most important of all is a feeling of **balance**. Many researchers are concentrating their efforts on understanding the vestibular system, including the inner ear and other neurological structures in an effort to help people with learning or physical problems of many varieties. It is vital to our functioning. That is why we often talk about wanting "more balance in our lives".

The concept of **emotion** is an interesting one; and sometimes causes a lot of confusion when people try to figure out what it really means. Emotions are a combination of things. Certainly we feel them, usually in many ways. They affect our sense of balance as well as temperature, pressure on certain areas of our bodies, and our sense of position (proprioception). But until we attach some *meaning* to these feelings, there really isn't an *emotion*. See the note **FEELINGS: KINESTHETICS & EMOTIONS** opposite for more explanation.

Often, becoming aware of our feelings is a powerful experience for people. Feelings have a special place in our behavior and some of these qualities of feeling seem to be the deciding factors in the overall quality of our experiences and our lives.

Olfactory and Gustatory Sub-Modalities

Though we don't usually think about them as much, smells and tastes can have a strong effect on our feelings. Just thinking about the way we use them in our everyday language says something about how we feel when we conjure up specific tastes and smells. For example, have you ever had an experience that "left a bitter taste in your mouth"? Ever become "soured on an experience"? Tasted the "sweet smell of success"? We wouldn't talk about what a "wonderful bitter time" we had, would we? Or the "sweet taste of disaster"? Those phrases don't make sense because our brains don't put things together that way. Remember, if it is built into our language in a specific way, it has just as specific a function in our thinking and experience. Here is a list of the common olfactory and gustatory sub-modalities.

Olfactory Sub-Modalities	**Gustatory Sub-Modalities**
Sweet	Pungent
Sour	Intensity
Salty	Location
Bitter	Aromatic
Specific taste	Specific smell

FEELINGS: KINESTHETICS & EMOTIONS

Everyone talks about emotions, but I find most people have only a vague idea of what they are actually talking about. In asking the question, "What is an emotion?", of many groups of people, the same kinds of confusion continually arise. Once people understand what emotion really is, and how it works, it seems to help enormously in solving problems.

First we need to understand feeling, the kinesthetic sense, itself. It breaks down into three separate but related categories:

Tactile: sense of touch on the surface of the skin (temperature, texture, moisture, physical contact, etc.)

Proprioceptive: sensation inside the body (internal pressure, tension, weight, body and limb relative position, etc.)

Vestibular: sense of balance (position in space, relationship to gravity, etc.)

Certainly, a strong emotion includes elements of each of these kinds of senses, but it is still more than that. We can have similar physical sensations in very different states, and therefore call these by different names. For example, think of the state commonly called the "fight or flight" condition (technical name: the *general adaptation syndrome*), in which you are totally physically mobilized for action. It includes a rush of adrenaline, extreme alertness to sights and sounds from the outside, and more. It is a preparation state for dangerous situations, giving us the energy and alertness we need to protect ourselves. But it comes up in a variety of situations. For example, an athlete might purposely produce it before an event to perform at his or her best. But in other situations, a phobic response, a quick avoidance of a car accident, a rage reaction to some perceived attack, we often automatically produce the same *physical* state. The athlete may label this state as "psyched up" or a "great rush". It's usually a highly enjoyable experience. In any of the other situations, however, this state is usually quite unpleasant and most of us wish we could avoid it.

So the context or situation in which we have this physical response will determine what we call it. And how we respond to it. If we want the state we enjoy it, if we don't we hate it. Same physiology, different *interpretation*.

An emotion is the combination of the physical (kinesthetic) sensations and the label (interpretation) we give it. This is based on the context. In fact, without the interpretation, it isn't even an emotion–it has no *meaning*. We need that conscious mind judgment to go along with the feelings to make something into an emotion. Excitement and fear are easy to confuse. It depends on how we *think* about it. That's the point to much of what we're doing in this book.

Solution States

The three main (visual, auditory and kinesthetic) lists of sub-modalities taken together, are a description of the major parts that comprise a state of consciousness. If you can identify as many of these as possible at a certain time, you will have a good description of your state of consciousness at that time. Adding in any olfactory or gustatory awarenesses can act as icing on the cake.

A state is like any other system. If you change one part, you change the whole system. Therefore, changing sub-modalities changes states. In a sense, to use a somewhat oversimplified analogy, your brain is something like a computer. It can do many things exquisitely well. It can process information with fabulous precision, consistently and dependably. It cannot, *at an unconscious level*, make *value judgments* on that information, though. It can store it, alter it, and make generalizations from it. And it will do so based on the built-in processes and the rules it has learned. In other words it will delete, distort and generalize in whatever ways it has learned, by whatever rules. It is, therefore, a good idea to teach it *worthwhile* rules. Then use it wisely.

Comparing States

Wise use of your brain includes deciding which states of consciousness you want, when you want them, and what to do with them. The more you practice, the more control you'll have over your state. Also, the more you'll control your abilities. This includes the ability to solve problems.

We all know, at least on an intuitive level, that when we are embroiled in a problem, we are not in our best state. We are often worried, angry, disgusted, rigid, lacking in confidence and resources, or just plain worn out. That is no position to be in when you need creativity, judgement, and drive. In fact it is the kind of state that pretty well insures that you won't have any of those necessary qualities (that may be why you have the problem to begin with). To show you how the states compare, on paper, here is an experiment in looking at some "before" and "after" pictures (sounds & feelings).

Note: **Read through the instructions first, before actually doing the experiment.**

EXPERIMENT: BEFORE AND AFTER

Step 1:

Remember a time when you were able to solve a particularly sticky problem. Perhaps one that had you, and maybe other people, stumped for a long time (if you choose, you could use your currently chosen problem, instead of one you have solved for the first part of this exercise). Take yourself back to that time and place so that it is as if you are back there now, fully re-living the experience.

Step 2:

Now begin with how you felt *just before* you had solved it (or how you feel now with the problem you still have). Get this image clear in your mind, complete with sounds and feelings, smells and tastes.

Step 3:

Starting with this "before" image, fill out the sub-modality checklist overleaf (on the left side titled "BEFORE") while you view this image in your mind.

Make a note to yourself about each of the visual sub-modalities, each of the auditory sub-modalities, and each of the kinesthetics. Make a note about smells and tastes If you notice any. For some people it helps to start with the feelings, since these may be what you notice most at first. These notes can be as simple or personal as you like. Also, some of the items may not apply, so skip over those. It sometimes helps to give yourself a measure of comparison as well. For example, you may compare brightness to the brightness in the room you're in now. Then you could just put "brighter", "dimmer", or "the same".

Step 4:

Now take yourself just slightly forward in time and remember how you felt just at the moment or *immediately after* you actually *solved* this problem. If you are working on a problem you still have, for this part of the exercise, remember a *different one*–one that you solved. Get this image clear in your mind, complete with sounds and feelings and, if you notice any, smells and tastes, again fully re-living the experience.

Step 5:

Now fill out the checklist section for the "AFTER" image, just as you did before. When you are done, you'll have notes on these two very different states of consciousness.

Step 6:

Compare the two lists of notes you have just made. Because these two states are so different, these images are probably very different in the qualities listed. That's what you'd expect.

Notice which of the sub-modalities are most different between the before and after experiences. These may be the most **critical** for you to be aware of. They may also be a guide to help you make changes easily and quickly in the future.

Sub-Modality Checklist

VISUAL	BEFORE	AFTER
Brightness		
Distance		
Size		
Shape		
Location/Direction		
Contrast		
Clarity		
Color		
Slide/Motion picture		
Movement/Speed		
Associated/Disassociated		
3-D (Depth)/Flat		
Focus		
Frame/No Frame		

AUDITORY		
Sound/Words		
Location		

Pitch _____ _____

Tone _____ _____

Voice/Whose? _____ _____

Distance _____ _____

Rhythm _____ _____

Timbre _____ _____

Internal/External _____ _____

Direction _____ _____

Tempo _____ _____

Volume _____ _____

Duration _____ _____

KINESTHETIC

Internal/External _____ _____

Location _____ _____

Weight _____ _____

Duration _____ _____

Size _____ _____

Pressure _____ _____

Frequency _____ _____

Tactile/Proprioceptive _____ _____

Shape _____ _____

Temperature _____ _____

Movement _____ _____

Intensity _____ _____

Moisture _____ _____

Texture _____ _____

Rhythm _____ _____

Balance _____ _____

Emotion _____ _____

OLFACTORY _____ _____

GUSTATORY _____ _____

For each of us there will be sub-modalities that are most **critical**. These are the ones that *make a big difference when we change them*. There may be others that have little effect on us, no matter how much we change them. This exercise should have given you a pretty good idea which ones are critical for you. If you concentrate on those, the rest should take care of themselves whenever you are trying to create a new state, or change the one you're in. You'll get plenty of practice as we continue.

Though the point to this is obvious, I want to repeat it again: If you have control over the states you go into, *you get to choose* which ones to have–ones that create problems, or ones that don't. The above exercise was a demonstration of how different these states can be from each other. We don't generally realize this until someone comes along to show us. The states you'll be developing to solve your problems will usually be very specific, just as the different types of problems we've identified are specific. Sometimes different problems require different kinds of solutions, developed from different kinds of states. There will also be some states that are generally useful, just as there are some that aren't.

CHAPTER 7

States Of Grace

No matter what kind of outcome you have chosen for yourself, you will need the most appropriate states to move forward and achieve it. These can be ones to solve problems, be motivated, make changes or any of a variety of others. Obviously, with the many different types of problems we've identified, there are many different kinds of states, sometimes several for each problem type, that could be helpful. Even beyond that, it's a really great personal development strategy to be able to generate, in yourself, a variety of different kinds of states, useful in different situations. It is true that flexibility is a major component of personal power and ability. This means flexibility in choosing the state most appropriate to any task.

Which states and where to find them

In using this model effectively, you can approach choosing your state in several ways. If you, for example, know that what you need is motivation, focus or creativity, you can simply remember a time when you were motivated, focused or creative. I'll take you through how to get into that state once you remember it, and be able to use it, in the next two chapters. Another approach that will work is to remember a time when you had a similar problem to the one you have now, but one that you were able to solve. In other words, pick a time when you had the same problem type as this one. Then get the state you used to *solve* that problem from your past experience (not the one you used to *have* the problem). Once you get into that state you'll have those *same resources* available again. I'll show you how to do that as well.

Another way to get a really good state for solving a problem, or anything else for that matter, is to do what the developers of NLP did: model someone. Essentially this would involve, first, choosing someone who has the *capability* that you want, for example someone who is good at solving the type of problem you have. Next, you would get hold of the person and find out as much information from them as you can. This would include what visual images this person has in mind when solving this kind of a problem, what he or she says inside his or her mind, and what feelings go along with these pictures and sounds. You could get this by asking good questions and through careful observations. Honestly, people tell you and show you these things all the time–it's knowing how to hear and see the information that takes practice.

Obviously, to do this kind of modeling in a formal and thorough way takes a good bit of training, and sufficient time with a willing subject. This is way beyond the scope of this book, but you might be surprised how well you can do just talking with someone about their experiences. When someone is really effective at something, they often love to talk about it, and in the process demonstrate how they go about doing it. You can pick up a tremendous amount of great information (conscious and unconscious) by paying close attention while they talk about themselves. A large number of public speakers, consultants and other experts will swear to you that the way to get more effective, and therefore successful, is to hang around people who already are. What makes this work is to be able to learn their thoughts, perceptions, and strategies from them. Most of this learning comes through unconscious modeling. In the next chapter we'll go through an exercise designed to help you model an ability, or state, someone else has.

Universally valuable states

There are states that will be useful, universally, in solving problems as well. For example, regardless of the type of problem you wish to solve, states like creativity, openness to change, focus of attention and motivation to succeed will always help you out. It may be that none of these is the one key to getting past your difficulty, but each will usually serve you well while you find and use whatever that special key might be. There are also states I think are useful to have in general, whether you are having a problem or not. Here is a variety of descriptions of various states that are helpful in not only solving problems in your business, but also in helping you become the kind of person you want to be.

Openness to Change

Sometimes people need to gear themselves up for change. In our culture, most of us learn that change is difficult and that it takes a long time. It really doesn't have to be that way. Often we make it much harder than it really is. Our opinions, beliefs and values usually are developed over long periods of time. So we are not likely to let go of them easily, because they took *work* to develop. Also, we often think that our beliefs and values have to be stable, if *we* are to be stable. This fear of being on shaky ground is usually what slows down the changes we need to make.

In NLP we have found that this shaky time can be quite exciting and growth producing–a time of real learning. In fact all learning is really change. If we think of it that way, it can actually be fun. There will certainly be times when it is difficult, but that should only be because we are learning and growing in really major and important ways that require our full attention and effort. If we can remove the fear, and concentrate on the learning, change can be wonderful. Having a state for enjoying the process of making change, and concentrating on the learning that goes with it, is really valuable.

Learning

While we're on the subject of learning, there are states that each of us has developed over our lifetimes that are useful for learning. In fact we have different states for learning different kinds of things. For example, we may have a state that is great for learning math, but lousy for learning how to get along with other people, and vice versa. States for learning various kinds of new information are always useful, and should be cultivated.

Taking Other Viewpoints: Perspective

Sometimes, for both change and learning, we need states that help us take on new points of view. This is often what allows us to take on new beliefs and understandings about how people and things work. This kind of flexibility in thinking is what ultimately determines maturity and wisdom.

The ability to recognize that everything changes when the context, or framework around it, changes, is of unquestionable value. Things don't always have the same meaning when viewed from different perspectives.

Creativity

Creativity comes in a variety of forms. That means a variety of states. There are "brainstorming" states in which you allow all your thoughts "air time" without censoring anything. This is a common method of gathering ideas in groups or teams. Any idea is acceptable while you are in this kind of a creative state–no matter how nuts it may look or sound on the surface.

Robert Dilts has studied creativity for many years. In fact he has studied the strategies of many brilliant people to discover which elements of their thinking we can all use–literal strategies of genius. One of the most useful of his studies has been the analysis of Walt Disney. It turns out, according to one of his animators, that Disney actually came in three varieties he called the dreamer, the realist, and the spoiler. Robert calls them the *dreamer*, the *realist* and the *critic*. Unfortunately for those who worked with Disney, they never knew which one they were going to run into next. You can probably imagine, just from those descriptive names that Walt, for all his genius, could be a bit difficult to predict, much less work with. Some would say that's part of the magic.

The idea of the dreamer, realist and critic is a great one though. We need to allow ourselves to dream, freely. By the same token we need to be able to look at what we're doing realistically. We also need to be self-critical to shape our ideas into something of quality. But we can't do all three *at the same time*. This is because each of these functions, as I hope you've already guessed, is the product of a different state. They need to be done separately, or the states will contaminate each other so that you can't do anything at all.

For example, how many times have you been with a group of people and someone came up with a really interesting idea for something (anything)? Then that person is interrupted in mid-sentence by someone else explaining all the reasons why it's stupid or unrealistic. It really shuts down the creativity fast, doesn't it? Most of the time it shuts everyone else up too. No one likes being blasted, and it's no way to be creative. It's a way to stifle creativity right out of existence. To be sure, we need to critically and realistically examine all proposals and ideas. But only after the creative process has been allowed to flourish. We'll come back to this later.

Another thing that will shoot creativity down is to insist that we don't have any. Many people don't realize that they are really creative, and in fact will vehemently argue the point (often quite *creatively*) until you give up and go along with them. While it's true that most of us recognize artists and other "creative types" as somehow gifted in this area, it doesn't follow that the rest of us don't have the same gift(s). Usually, we automatically create new things, or new thoughts, all the time without *recognizing* that we are doing it. We just need to focus on it while it's happening and notice how we did it, or at least notice the state we're in at the time.

For example, you may have combined two things (pieces of equipment, maybe) together that no one had thought of before, and made your life easier. You may have figured out a new time schedule for getting things done that worked brilliantly. Perhaps you came up with a streamlined procedure that other people couldn't see. Or found a way to deal with a difficult situation, or person, that helped you (or somebody) out of a jam. Maybe you dress in unusual and novel ways. When you make a salad at the salad bar, or a sandwich from leftovers, it comes out great and unique. A short cut to work. A new way to trim the hedges, cut the grass or plant a garden. A letter to a colleague or friend that made a difference. A way to save money on a vacation, a party, a new car or anything else, for that matter. The poetry to an old love, a story about a potato, or the three chord rock and roll song you wrote in high school that actually sounded different than the ones your friends wrote (a friend of mine won a national collegiate *poetry* contest with one of his old rock songs). The way you figured out that the butler didn't do it the last time you went to a movie or read a story. That one idea you came up with that actually convinced your children to do something that was good for them (probably to your own surprise and astonishment). The way that, even after reading this list, you cleverly decided you are the only exception in the world to my insistence that everyone is creative (if you find a way out of that one, it will prove, beyond the shadow of a doubt, that you're truly gifted in the area of creativity).

Focus

Obviously, there are times when we need to be highly focused and able to concentrate on the task at hand. That may not be what got us into our current problem, but it may be what we need to get out of it. We have all had times of extreme focus in our lives. For some of us it can even cause a problem. Have you ever been reading something so interesting that people have been talking to you, or even shouting at you, and you didn't notice until they came up and shook you out of your book? How about watching TV or a movie? Driving down a long road? Listening to music, or a great speech or lecture? Fishing? Daydreaming? Watching a campfire? Working on a small piece of equipment? Cooking a meal? These are examples of some of the most common things that take us away from "reality" and into our own little worlds. They are also examples of naturally occurring hypnosis in everyday life. We can use these for our benefit.

Planning, Setting Goals & Outcomes

We've spent so much time on setting goals and outcomes that it may seem needless to bring it up again. However, you may have discovered that there are times you do these things better than others. If so, then think about those times when you have done so especially well and identify the states. Then, along with the guidelines I've set out for you, and any others you may have learned, you'll have another good tool. Perhaps you have states that help you better organize your thinking, collect resources, plan or set priorities. These can all be very helpful as well.

Handling Constraints or Adversity

Perhaps you have some really great states for handling adversity. It will always be a part of life and business. We have all had to deal with it at some time, and we usually seem to get through and go on with our lives. Clearly we do better some times than others. We can harness those times and the resources that go with them and keep them at the ready.

An interesting example comes from, of all places, airline disasters. Studies have clearly shown that people who imagine, ahead of time, what they would do in an emergency are far more likely to survive if there is one. That means they actually rehearse in their minds the steps they would take and the direction they would go if they needed to. When it happens, they react much more quickly and automatically. The same can go for handling any kind of emergency or difficult situation. Planning should include planning for possible problems.

In a related manner, how do you handle major constraints on your planning and functioning? Being able to deal with limitations is really necessary since the world will never give you everything you want on time, in perfect working order, to exact specification, in unlimited quantity ... Right? There are given limitations in everything we do. The realist within each of us knows that. We should be able to access that realist to help us plan and act accordingly.

Breaking Habits

A lot of people are in the habit of thinking they can't do something–like be creative. That is a constraint that is unrealistic. More often, though, people do things that they don't even realize they're doing. All of us, at one time or another, have broken some habit, stopped some unwanted behavior or interrupted some compulsive action or obsessive thought by doing something else instead. The obvious bad habits we have are one thing, but the ones we don't notice are another.

So-called "efficiency experts" earlier this century often would begin a study of some plant or organization by carefully observing every motion workers went through ("time-motion studies"). These observations were often of the smallest details you could imagine. The point was to figure out which motions people went through were useful (toward getting the product out) and which were just wasted effort. Some of this was helpful, some was just plain silly.

The idea behind observing someone's behavior, or your own, is a good one, no matter what the findings. An exercise that management consultants have been recommending for years is to make careful notes about what you actually do during the day, in small time segments. For example, break each hour down into ten minute segments, and make notes about what you are actually doing in each one. Then, when you look at the results, over a period of time, you can find things you do that are worthless in *your* opinion. *You* get to decide which things to keep, or not.

Sometimes it takes a state of real diligence to notice what you are doing. Sometimes it takes even more to consciously do something else instead. We'll come back to this later.

This, of course, doesn't mean you can't ask for help or advice, or for someone to point out any habits they think you should gracefully lose. If you have managed to surround yourself with people you trust, they can be of great help. If you need to get yourself into some particular state in which to ask them for help, or listen to it when they give it, you can only improve as a person. It may take guts, but, if you trust people, trust them. Defensiveness in this case is just not a worthwhile state.

Taking Action, Motivation

If you find that you sometimes know what to do, but just don't do it, then perhaps you could use a state for taking action. Some people stay stuck in the state of planning, rather than ever doing. In this case it might be that what you need is to get out of the state you're in first, and then into the one you need; nearly always the case.

There is certainly a variety of states you could develop for motivation, or even *compulsion*. Compulsiveness isn't necessarily bad. We all do things compulsively that we would be foolish to stop. Think about brushing your teeth in the morning, saying hello to people, shaking hands when you meet someone new, fastening your seat belt before you drive and cleaning up your home (car, office or whatever) when you can no longer walk through the room. These social, safety and convenience compulsions are good for us. Some of them we do better than others. Why not pick one or two that you do well, and are glad you have, and examine how the state works? Then you could use that state for lots of other things you wish you would do just as automatically.

Beyond that, some people need specific states to help them carry something through to completion, instead of stopping near the end. As a writer, I know that the last 10% of the work can take 50% of the time. That is overwhelming for many people, and keeps them from ever getting to the end. I simply plan for it. Sometimes what people need is a little more ambition. Sometimes a little more feeling for the value of success. Or a passion. You can develop states for any of these.

Willingness to Take Risks

If fear stops you, it could be that the fear is stronger than the desire to succeed. In that case, perhaps thinking back to times you overcame fears and doubts could be of great help. It could also be that trying new things, accepting challenges or taking risks is something you shy away from. You've done all of these things before. All functioning people have. Remembering some times when you did something that seemed risky, but it worked out well, could help you now. This certainly doesn't mean to take risks just for the sake of daring, however. Everyone is presented with opportunities for growth and success that seem genuinely promising to them. Those are the ones worth going for.

Feeling Safe & Secure

Conversely, feeling safe and secure is something we all need some of the time. Often it is what we need before we can take those worthwhile risks we want to take. And we've all felt safe and secure at some point in our lives, even if it was only in our bedroom when we were kids (or under the bed for that matter). People should be able to create security for themselves, but it obviously has to start inside of themselves. Remembering a safe place is a good start. Then you can add feelings of being capable, intelligent and resourceful to add to your security. In fact, if you have those things, you can make your own security.

Decision Making

You have to be able to make decisions to solve problems. Hopefully, good ones. We've all made thousands of decisions in our lives, about thousands of different things. We've learned a lot from them. Now we can also *learn from the process of making them*, not just the results. Pick some decisions you made that worked out well, and some that worked out badly. Examine them and discover if there was a difference in the *way* you made the decision. As we discussed in the section on Audience, there are many different ways people make decisions, based on a variety of factors. If you look back over the questions I asked you about Convincers, Motivators and Thinking Style, you may see a pattern in the way you decide things. Perhaps each time you've made a good decision you've paid attention to more of the factors involved than when you made decisions that didn't turn out so well.

Also, it may be that you have a state that works extremely well for you when you need to decide something. If you can identify it, you can learn to use it much more often. It could be that you have a state that allows you to step back from what you're thinking about and see it from a different perspective, or in a different framework. Maybe you have one that helps you remember sage advice you've heard in the past that could be applied now. Maybe you can really tune in to your gut reaction, and you've found that this is reliable in some situations. All of these methods are equally viable. Some you will do better than others. They're worth identifying.

Clarity and Understanding

It may sound strange, but we have optimal states for comprehending, understanding and knowing things. Sometimes we're just more clear-headed than at other times. Sometimes we need to be in a particular state for understanding certain kinds of information, just like we need for learning some things. These can be closely related to one another, and equally worthwhile exploring.

Developing Effective Relationships
Gaining & Maintaining Rapport

Relationships are obviously very important to all of us, whether at home or at work. For many of us, they influence most of what we do. Just as we can have strategies for approaching others, asking for help or feedback about something, or solving problems with others, we can have states in which we are better at all of these things. These may include being able to take the point of view of another person or even the way they understand something. It may include a willingness to look at our own behavior, listen to criticism, or control or better express real feelings. Sometimes it takes an understanding of the natural changes and progressions that relationships go through in their evolution. Other times we need to notice, somehow see and hear, that roles have changed in some way (or that they haven't, but should).

There is, of course, no limit to the skills involved in having good relationships with others. All of them start with willingness and a belief that they are worthwhile and important. Then, the right state for understanding, appreciating, accepting, or communicating with others is what will make our living and working with them fruitful. If we are in a state of rapport with those we have to deal with, we can always develop the relationship into what we want and need. Without good rapport, we're stuck hoping the other person will go along with what we want, but with no way to work together toward our common interests.

Being Healthy

Often people don't take as much time to consider their physical well-being as they should. If you are one of those people, on some level you probably know it. Are there times when you take really good care of yourself? Other times when you don't? What is the difference? How much of that difference is due to outside factors, and how much is strictly your own responsibility (be honest, now)? What states do you get into that automatically drive you toward taking the best care of your health that you can? What can you do to optimize those?

If you don't already know it, you'd be surprised how much of our thinking is governed by our diet, exercise, rest and sleep and general health. All of the states we get into are affected by these things. It is up to us to be aware of them and take good care of ourselves. In fact, there is no excuse anymore for not taking the responsibility to be as healthy as possible. There is just too much good information and help available.

141

Finishing

Finally, for our list, we have the notion of *finishing*. Some people never quite feel they have accomplished something. Or they can't let go of a task, problem or project. Sometimes they can't let go of a relationship or a goal either. There is something almost mystical about the letting go process. I know writers who are never finished (we all know people like that). Others finish their work but never send it to anyone, or let anyone know they've completed what they set out to do.

Sometimes the problem is that all the excitement is in the work itself. This is great for motivation, lousy for a sense of accomplishment or completion. For some people more of a problem is moving on to something new. They may have enjoyed, or felt secure in what they were doing, to the point that they don't want to stop. Sometimes finishing means no longer working in a place (or with certain people) that makes us feel good and successful.

There are no easy answers to any of these things. All of us, though, have accomplished things, said good-bye to people and places–and moved on. We've all left jobs, school and projects when we were done. That means we all have the memories and experiences we need to get the states that have been useful to us. They can ease the pain, help us adjust, and move us in new and more profitable directions if we simply use them.

Undoubtedly you could come up with lots of other kinds of states you would like to have in addition to the ones I've described here. Hopefully, you're thinking about your own work, and life, and how to make it better. There is almost no limit to the ways we can use our memories, experiences and abilities to make us better at everything we do. It is our responsibility as adults to do so. The next two chapters will teach you how.

CHAPTER 8

Designer States

Now that you know how states are built, and what kind of influence changing them can really have, it's time to start designing ones we can use to solve our problems. Obviously, with the many different categories of problems we explored earlier, along with the listing in the last chapter, there is a variety of different states we can develop. At the end of the first section you had identified which type you were working on, so that may be the one you wish to start with. We are going to go through developing several that are most universally useful, from each of the categories. Though they won't all necessarily be applicable for you now, they probably will be at some time in the future. Also, as you read through the descriptions, as well as doing the exercises, you'll learn a great deal about how problems come up and what to do about them.

My intention is to actually guide you through building a "designer state" for whatever kind of problem you are having, or even ones you anticipate in the future. This will be determined by the type of problem you've identified. You'll build this state out of other states you have been in before. There are several ways of getting the states we need. The four basic ones are:

1. Vividly remembering a time when you were in that specific state that you now need;
2. Remembering a time when you solved a similar problem (which assumes you had the state to do it in);
3. Artificially designing the state or building it from similar states;
4. Modeling it from someone else.

The first way, as I've said, is to vividly remember a time when we had the specific state we want, as if we were there again. This is what you did earlier when you retrieved your state of excitement and enthusiasm. Sometimes, though, we aren't sure exactly which state we need. If that's the case, the second method, using our memory to bring back a state in which we solved a similar problem to the one we have, is a good way to go. This is what you did when you compared the states you had before and after solving a past problem. The third way is to remember a state similar to the one we need, and then adjust the sub-modalities until we have what we want. This can be called an artificially designed state. It still relies on conjuring up a set of images and feelings from our past that we think are useful, like the other two methods. In fact, there is every good reason to adjust any state we get into so that it is the strongest or most effective it can be.

The fourth way we can get a state is to get it from someone else, through modeling. As I said earlier, this takes training and time to do thoroughly, but it can be done, well enough in most instances, even without these. You can do this if you have some access to the person you're modeling, or that you know this person well enough that you understand, at least on an unconscious level, how he or she operates. If you have been around this person while they were performing the task you want to learn, then you probably got enough from them to be able to do this. (I wish there were a more perfect way of deciding, but other methods are way beyond the scope of this book. For now, you'll have to rely on the results of the procedure to tell you if you know the person well enough unconsciously).

Modeling is really the most powerful learning tool there is and it comes in several forms. The one here is the easiest and safest to use. It is called the "As If Frame" and was developed by John Grinder in the early days of NLP. It's a way of accessing all your unconscious knowledge about another person, and their abilities and resources. You will actually imagine that you can "step inside" the person you wish to model. Because of this, there are a few cautions I want you to observe while you do so.

1. Be sure that this person really has the talent, ability or state that you want to have. Not just that they say so, or someone else says so. You should have an actual *demonstration*, or have already seen and heard them do what you want to be able to do, before you believe that they have this talent.

2. Make sure that you take only the resources you n[e]
from modeling this person. You don't really want to
become a "clone" of anyone else, no matter how much
you might admire their abilities in one particular area.
If you know the person well enough, you probably
know their blemishes as well. You don't want *those*,
just their talents.
3. You may have to do this several times to get it right.
You also may have to observe this person you choose
after you've tried it; you may find some gaps in your
knowledge.
4. You may find yourself doing, or thinking, things that
do not fit with who you are as a person, or your basic
beliefs and values. If so, fine. Be aware of them as you
go through the following exercise, and each time you
repeat it.

These are important things to be aware of and considered.
Finally, the only way to know if you have done this well is to
test it. You will either have more of the ability you want, or
not. If you do, great. If not, you may need to do it again, or
do something else instead.

EXPERIMENT: BORROWING TALENT

Step 1:
Pick a resource you would like to have. This could be an
ability, it could be a behavior, a skill, some knowledge, a
particular kind of resource or a state. It could be a state
you think you need, or an ability you believe you could use,
to solve a problem; either the one you have identified, or
another. You may decide there are several of these that
you would like. If so, you may want to do this experiment
several times.
Alternatively, you may be able to think of a single person
who exhibits everything that you want, for this purpose.

Step 2:
Choose a person you believe has this resource, or all of
these resources, fully available to them. This will undoubtedly be someone who exhibits true *excellence* in this
instance. *Never model mediocrity.*

I need to stress that you pick what you want first, and then decide who has it, rather than just picking someone who intrigues or impresses you in general. Be specific about what you want, and then about who has exactly that.

Step 3:
Imagine that this other person is in front of you, doing what it is that you want to be able to do. In other words, this person is actually performing what they are excellent at, in the state they use to be excellent at it.

Step 4:
Now imagine that you can take this person's place in this image before you. "Step into" the picture and *act as if you are this person*. Do what they do, feel what they feel, think what they think, while they are in this highly resourceful state, doing what you want to be able to do. Enjoy it.

Step 5:
Pay attention to how you act as this person, as opposed to how you normally would act in this situation. These differences are the result of that other person's resources and talents.

You might imagine how you would handle your own difficulties, or solve your problem, right now, as this other person. Imagine carrying through on the outcome you want, if that is appropriate, and what it would be like.

Decide how you like this new behavior. What would you like to keep? Is there anything you would rather not have, or do, that you find yourself doing as this person? What fits, and what doesn't–for you?

Step 6:
Notice what is special and different about this state. What images do you have in your mind while you act as if you were this other person? What do you hear in your mind, or say to yourself? How does it feel? Are there any smells or tastes that you are aware of?

Step 7:
Fill out the DESIGNER STATE WORK SHEET below according to the following instructions.

On the top line called Descriptive Label, put down the name of the person   you have chosen to model. On the lines called Description of Content, make a note about what the ability you have borrowed from this person is, and how you wish to use it.

Ignore the last line labeled Description of Anchor–we'll come back to that later. Then jot a note down next to any sub-modalities that you find unusual or different for you as you act this out.

Take your time doing this, and make sure that you are really in the state where you feel effective while you do.

Step 8:

Go back to being yourself. Ask yourself what it was like being as if you were someone else, and if there are things you learned that were unexpected.

DESIGNER STATE WORK SHEET

Descriptive Label_____

Description of Content_____

_____

_____

VISUAL

Brightness	_____	Focus	_____
Distance	_____	Slide	_____
Size	_____	Motion Picture	_____
Shape	_____	Movement/Speed	_____
Location	_____	Associated	_____
Direction	_____	Disassociated	_____
Contrast	_____	Depth 3D/Flat	_____
Clarity	_____	Frame/No Frame	_____
Color	_____	Other?	_____

Solution States

AUDITORY

Sounds	_____	Timbre	_____
Words	_____	Internal	_____
Location	_____	External	_____
Pitch	_____	Direction	_____
Tone	_____	Tempo	_____
Voice (Who?)	_____	Volume	_____
Distance	_____	Duration	_____
Rhythm	_____	Other?	_____

KINESTHETIC

Internal	_____	Proprioceptive	_____
External	_____	Shape	_____
Location	_____	Temperature	_____
Weight	_____	Movement	_____
Duration	_____	Intensity	_____
Size	_____	Moisture	_____
Pressure	_____	Texture	_____
Frequency	_____	Rhythm	_____
Tactile	_____	Balance	_____
Emotion?	_____	Other?	_____

OLFACTORY/GUSTATORY

Sweet	_____	Pungent	_____
Sour	_____	Intensity	_____
Salty	_____	Location	_____
Bitter	_____	Aromatic	_____
Specific taste	_____	Specific smell	_____

Description of Anchor_____

_____

This modeling exercise can be a very powerful experience if you engage in it fully. It can also provide you with a lot of ability you may not have believed you would ever have. In fact, you'll know you did it really well if, during the time you imagined you were this other person, you seemed to have knowledge and abilities that came "out of the blue". That is a common experience. Or, all of a sudden understanding a problem or goal from a different perspective. Or new ideas "popping" into your head, all of a sudden. Or automatically behaving in ways you never would have thought to behave. These are all descriptions I've heard from people doing this for the first (second, third and so on) time.

Caution is necessary, however. We can pick up bad habits from people very easily. This kind of exercise makes it even easier. Remember to ask yourself about whether the new ideas and behavior you learned fit with who you are as a person. You might even look over your notes from the earlier sections of the book to make sure.

I would also emphasize that the main advantage to this exercise is in learning to do things that others do well. Most of the time, getting into the states we need is far easier than this. We nearly always have been in the states we need before, and need only use our memories of those earlier times to get there again. Save this modeling experiment for special learning and changes you need to make. Or when you know that your experience in a particular area is so limited that "tapping into" the resources of a "mentor" would be valuable. Also, ask this person for help, directly, if they are available.

A note on the Designer State Work Sheet. This is a tool you'll be using from now on. It will be handy if you make copies, or photocopies, since you will need several. Also, you may decide that it is something you will want to use regularly–photocopy a stack of them now for later use. I designed them as a convenient way to code an entire state on one page, complete with a label, content description, sub-modalities and more. Once you have filled one out, it will make it much easier to get into that state again, just by using the sheet. I'll explain how in the next chapter. Also, this is very similar to what the computer will do with you, should you decide to use the technology of the NeuroLink (see the appendix section for more information).

Specific States for Specific Problem Types

Let's take another look at the list of problem types from Chapter 5.

1. Personal (individual) problems
    a) Creativity/Innovation
    b) Motivation
    c) Focus
    d) Planning, productivity & limitations
    e) Tools, materials, support, time/space
    f) Neuro-logical levels

2. Interpersonal/Communication problems
    a) Vision
    b) Intention
    c) Clarity, Understanding
    d) Rapport
    e) Objections

3. Training problems
    a) Training effectiveness
    b) Knowledge, Skills & Procedures
    c) Systemic effects
    d) Neuro-logical level effects

4. Systemic problems
    a) Design flaws & communication
    b) Timing & System reverberation

5. Environmental/Situational problems

Personal (individual) problems

It is important to remember that everyone in business is a person first, and a *business* person (salesperson, CEO, secretary, manager, supervisor, etc.) *second*. This should go without saying at this point but, like most things, it is better off said anyway. That's why we begin with designing states that concentrate on Personal (individual) problems.

As we look over the list, we can see that some of these types of problems will be easy to solve simply by getting into a particular state. For example, if our problem is caused by our personal lack of motivation, it could be quite easy, using what we've discussed so far, to simply remember a time we were highly motivated, and get that state. This, in fact, will usually work just fine. The same might go for creativity, innovation and focus. If a lack of the right state is the actual problem itself, then the state is all we need.

Sometimes a personal business problem could be a matter of organizing, in your mind, what it is you actually do. From the many questions you answered earlier, you have undoubtedly been thinking about this a great deal. An example is in order, though. When people ask me what *I* do, I tell them I work on projects (outcomes). A project could be a training program, a research project, a consultation, a seminar, a book, article or paper, a special meeting or any of several other things. This perspective makes it easy for me to see a start and finish to each thing I do. When people ask, "But aren't you an author (speaker, trainer, researcher, consultant, etc.)?" I say, "Sure, sometimes, but that *isn't the way I think about it.*" In writing a book, it is easier to think about a chapter at a time, or even a section of a chapter, than the whole thing. It is, in the same way, easier to imagine completing a project than it is to have to view a whole career at once. That's not to say that the "Big Picture" isn't useful. It's just a matter of *when.* There are clearly limits to how much any of us can handle at one time. Using that knowledge can keep us focused on the level of analysis we need to be focused on.

Sometimes personal business problems involve judgments about the *quality* of one's work, or the *desirability* of doing a particular thing. Again, these are valid concerns. Ones that need to be carefully considered. There are times when most of us ask ourselves if we are really doing what we want to be doing. That's a good question regardless of what the answer is (or even if we don't have an answer). We're all people first and business people second.

MASTERIES

We like to focus on both knowledge and skills in NLP, and which skills people need so that we can figure out how to better develop them. In this sense, Robert Dilts and Gino Bonissone have identified four essential *masteries* effective business and organizational leaders will need in the future:

1. Relevance
2. Thoroughness
3. Balance
4. Meta-Cognition

Relevance is clearly important, especially in organizational life because we have to know what things to focus on to get things done. What matters. And there is way too much for us to handle without having the ability to pull out essential features of any situation that we can directly affect. Information overload makes it necessary for us to narrow down our search for solutions to the relevant pieces.

Thoroughness in this sense means *finishing* what we start rather than leaving any important job only partly done. We all get bogged down in our work from time to time and try to get through doing things as quickly as possible; just to relieve the pressure of overload. But some of those quick patches will come apart later and leave us with an even bigger mess. We need to be thorough, test our effectiveness, insure that our decisions are followed all the way through to completion and constantly beware of unfinished business that can come back to haunt us.

Balance is something most of us strive for, but find hard to manage. This is especially true when we feel as if we are juggling too many balls at once. In business this means paying attention to the most important things, and avoiding getting caught giving all of our time to some areas at the expense of others; especially those that will cause us problems later. All of us, at some times get too over- focused and let certain things go, even areas of our personal lives. In some cases it *is* our personal life we let go. Family, relationships, health (diet, rest, exercise), continuing education and learning, personal interests and other areas of our lives are important. For most of us, those are the things we work so hard for. Ignoring them is perilous.

Finally, *meta- cognition* will become more and more crucial. It means "thinking about thinking." For our purposes in this book it means specifically paying close attention to *how we are thinking when we are doing it*. In other words, noticing the images we have in our mind, the things we say to ourselves and how we feel— moment to moment. The exercises in this book, especially those in Part II, are designed in part to help focus attention inward to help in this process. In the future, *how* we think will become as important as *what* we think. The more we become aware of our own thinking processes, the more we can improve and refine them. Essential.

If the problem is the direct result of needing a particular state, then simply remember the last time you were in that state and go to it. It may be, however, that the problem you've identified, and the outcome you have designed, don't rely on something as simple as getting motivated, creative or focused. Perhaps you have identified a personal/individual problem that requires dealing with certain kinds of limitations in time or materials, or requires some special kind of support or changes in planning. There will, still, be *some states that allow you to handle these* better than others. Regardless of the specific kind of problem, the next experiment should help you get an optimal state for tackling it.

EXPERIMENT: DESIGNER STATE FOR PERSONAL BUSINESS PROBLEMS

Step 1:

Remember a time when you were faced with a problem of the same type as the one you now wish to solve. In other words, one that was of the same category of personal (individual) problem as this one. If you are not now working on a problem of this type, it will be most worthwhile to remember solving a problem that required you to be in a state of creativity/innovation, motivation or focus since these will be useful for you regardless.

Once you have remembered a particular problem of this type, imagine that you can go back in time to the *exact moment* when you found or developed the *solution* to this problem. This may have been the moment you came to a specific decision, or changed your point of view about what you were doing in your work.

Note: Experience, and logic, teaches us that at this moment when you developed the solution, you were *in the state you needed* to do so. That is why you need to get this exact moment–and exact state.

Jot down notes on the DESIGNER STATE WORK SHEET on the next page. On the Descriptive Label line, put the problem type that this memory fits. On the Description of Content lines, put down the time you are remembering and whatever notes you need so that, later, when you look at this again, you will remember where it came from.

Step 2:

While you are remembering the feelings that go with this decision or change in your view, fill out the KINESTHETIC portion of the sheet.

Step 3:

Now carefully examine whatever internal visual image, or images, you have in this state. Fill out the VISUAL portion of the sheet now.

Step 4:

Now, again, listen to the sounds you have in your mind especially your own voice as you talk to yourself about how you've solved the problem, changed in some way or come to the resolution of this difficulty. You may remember the voices of other people as well, perhaps giving you some special sage advice in this respect. When you can clearly hear all that is going on in your mind, fill out the AUDITORY portion of the sheet.

Step 5:

If you are aware of any outstanding smells or tastes as you experience this state, make notes about those now as well.
Note: For now, continue to leave the last line, Description of Anchor, blank.

DESIGNER STATE WORK SHEET

Descriptive Label_____

Description of Content_____

_____

_____

VISUAL

Brightness	_____	Focus	_____
Distance	_____	Slide	_____
Size	_____	Motion Picture	_____
Shape	_____	Movement/Speed	_____
Location	_____	Associated	_____
Direction	_____	Disassociated	_____

Contrast	_____	Depth 3D/Flat	_____
Clarity	_____	Frame/No Frame	_____
Color	_____	Other?	_____

AUDITORY

Sounds	_____	Timbre	_____
Words	_____	Internal	_____
Location	_____	External	_____
Pitch	_____	Direction	_____
Tone	_____	Tempo	_____
Voice (Who?)	_____	Volume	_____
Distance	_____	Duration	_____
Rhythm	_____	Other?	_____

KINESTHETIC

Internal	_____	Proprioceptive	_____
External	_____	Shape	_____
Location	_____	Temperature	_____
Weight	_____	Movement	_____
Duration	_____	Intensity	_____
Size	_____	Moisture	_____
Pressure	_____	Texture	_____
Frequency	_____	Rhythm	_____
Tactile	_____	Balance	_____
Emotion?	_____	Other?	_____

OLFACTORY/GUSTATORY

Sweet	_____	Pungent	_____
Sour	_____	Intensity	_____
Salty	_____	Location	_____
Bitter	_____	Aromatic	_____
Specific taste	_____	Specific smell	_____

Description of Anchor_____

_____

There are people who would argue that all problems in business are personal problems of the type I've described, or at the very least have these as a major underlying component. Probably true. This isn't always the best way to think through the problem to solutions, though I would support starting with yourself whenever you encounter a problem, just as we have here. The worst thing that could happen is that you'll clarify your own role, and be sure what responsibility belongs to you, and how much belongs to others.

Interpersonal/Communication Problems

In my experience the majority of complaints people make in business are complaints about other people. People problems seem to dominate the literature, the workshop, seminar, and consulting business, and even the popular press. Since business is people, this isn't surprising. What is surprising is that so many people seem to find dealing with others so difficult, when it should be so natural. Oh well.

What I want to focus on now are the kinds of problems between people that drive us to distraction–and I mean that literally. How many times have you heard yourself say, "If I have to put up with that !@#$%^&* (person) one more time I'm going to ...!" We've all said things like that, probably too often. And probably *thought* them even more. The real problem is that we are driven so much to distraction, that we are distracted from our own good sense and our resources for getting along with others.

We need to appreciate likenesses and differences between ourselves and other people. Likenesses are what bring us together, help us establish rapport, and allow us to understand one another. Differences are what make us unique, creative in various ways, and complementary in our abilities. If we think about it honestly, most of us wouldn't want to be surrounded with clones of ourselves. In fact some of us find enough trouble with just one of ourselves in the world. I've heard some people in business, after seeing the power of NLP in helping people duplicate the high level performance of others, actually complain that they are afraid that the technology would indeed make clones of their employees–taking away their individuality. The funny part is when they complain that their problems are the result of a lack of uniformity of performance. Odd. The point is that there obviously needs to be a balance between doing things in a consistent way, and enough individuality to lend creativity, alternative choices, style and flair where it is needed.

Rapport is crucial. We must have some rapport with those we deal with to get along, understand, and appreciate one another. How much rapport depends on the tasks. How much lack of rapport can be tolerated depends on the people. There are lots of ways of establishing and maintaining rapport but the important thing is that you do it, regardless of how. Rapport means a sense of understanding, trust, and a shared sense of values and purpose. The more you have, the better you work with those around you.

Again, we know that everyone who is at all successful in business has had to deal effectively with some difficult people. Most of them learned how *in life* first, but not all. Some learned on the job. We can use the same kind of creative ways of dealing with others (provided that we get into good creative states first). You wouldn't want to do exactly the same thing with everyone each time you encounter some difficulty, but you may be able to use the same kind of creativity to come up with unique ways of handling unique people. It is the creative state, in which you understand and appreciate peoples' uniqueness, that will allow you to find or develop new ways to handle people problems.

Remember that we have isolated common interpersonal and communication problems that come down to:

1. Lack of a shared vision;
2. Unclear intentions on your part or others';
3. Lack of clarity or understanding;
4. A general lack of rapport; or
5. Some objections that have not been properly addressed.

We have all experienced problems like these in some area of our lives, if not at work. No matter what type of communication problem you have experienced, or are experiencing now, you have also communicated well many more times in your life with other people. Maybe even with the person or people you're having difficulty with now. That is the important thing to remember. Somewhere in your past experience, you've solved this kind of problem and communicated effectively with others.

EXPERIMENT: DESIGNER STATE FOR INTER-PERSONAL/COMMUNICATION PROBLEMS

Step 1:
Think back to a time when you were having a problem with someone, or even several people in your work. If this is the current problem you are having, think of a time when you had as similar a problem as you can remember. Imagine, that you can go back in time to the exact moment when you found or developed the solution to this problem, just as you did in the last exercise, on personal problems.

In other words, what happened in your mind that allowed you to deal with these people in a different way? What new understanding about their needs, goals, or motivations occurred to you that made you see things from their point of view? What did you say to yourself, or hear them say, that sparked your understanding and appreciation of this, or these other peoples' uniqueness? This may have been a moment you came to a specific decision, let go of some personal pride or anger, or just knew that if you did something different, they would too. How did you communicate in a new and more effective way?

Jot down notes on the DESIGNER STATE WORK SHEET on the next page. On the Descriptive Label line, put the problem type that this memory fits. On the Description of Content lines, put down the time you are remembering and whatever notes you need so that, later, when you look at this again, you will remember where it came from.

Step 2:
While you are remembering the feelings that go with this decision, change in viewpoint, or new understanding fill out the KINESTHETIC portion of the sheet.

Step 3:
Now carefully examine whatever internal visual image, or images, you have while you're in this state. Fill out the VISUAL portion of the sheet now.

Step 4:
Now, again, listen to the sounds you have in your mind especially your own voice as you talk to yourself about this

change you made. You may remember specific conversations that occurred at that time. When you can clearly hear all that you need, fill out the AUDITORY portion of the sheet.

DESIGNER STATE WORK SHEET

Descriptive Label_____

Description of Content_____

_____

_____

VISUAL

Brightness	_____	Focus	_____
Distance	_____	Slide	_____
Size	_____	Motion Picture	_____
Shape	_____	Movement/Speed	_____
Location	_____	Associated	_____
Direction	_____	Disassociated	_____
Contrast	_____	Depth 3D/Flat	_____
Clarity	_____	Frame/No Frame	_____
Color	_____	Other?	_____

AUDITORY

Sounds	_____	Timbre	_____
Words	_____	Internal	_____
Location	_____	External	_____
Pitch	_____	Direction	_____
Tone	_____	Tempo	_____
Voice (Who?)	_____	Volume	_____
Distance	_____	Duration	_____
Rhythm	_____	Other?	_____

Solution States

KINESTHETIC

Internal	_____	Proprioceptive	_____
External	_____	Shape	_____
Location	_____	Temperature	_____
Weight	_____	Movement	_____
Duration	_____	Intensity	_____
Size	_____	Moisture	_____
Pressure	_____	Texture	_____
Frequency	_____	Rhythm	_____
Tactile	_____	Balance	_____
Emotion?	_____	Other?	_____

OLFACTORY/GUSTATORY

Sweet	_____	Pungent	_____
Sour	_____	Intensity	_____
Salty	_____	Location	_____
Bitter	_____	Aromatic	_____
Specific taste	_____	Specific smell	_____

Description of Anchor_____

_____

This is an area in which modeling others can be particularly helpful. When we are having a problem communicating with, or getting along with, someone else, it is easy for us to get caught thinking that that person is just not able to communicate or get along with others. But there is undoubtedly *someone* that this person *does* get along with. You probably know who, too. Ask yourself how this other person manages to get through to the one you're having a hard time with–it can make all the difference. Or ask them. Or simply observe. If something is possible in the world, it's possible for you. That means if *anyone* can communicate with this "problem" person, so can you.

That is really what people problems are about–realizing that there is always a way for people to get along. Also, realizing how central it is to the other things that have to be accomplished. Then, making it happen, in a way in which everyone feels that they are taken seriously, considered as people and as workers.

Training Problems

Often, what appear on the outside to be personal or inter-personal problems are really related to training. The very best training really provides people with the kinds of tools and knowledge we discussed under both of those categories. I believe that people often have to get their motivation, creativity, sense of focus, planning and the rest while they are training in their job. Much as we would like to get people gifted with these to begin with, more often these gifts have to be trained in. The same goes for interpersonal skills, communication and rapport.

If you have determined that your problem falls into the area of training, there are several things you need to think about.

1. What specific knowledge or skills do the people involved (including you) need?
2. Do you know how or where to get this training?
3. What will be the effects of implementing this training on the people involved (time away from their other tasks, the meta-messages of asking them to get training, the feelings of others around them, etc.)?
4. Most importantly, what is their readiness to accept training, learn, and make changes? Anyone not in the best state to learn and make changes is wasting valuable time and energy in a training course, regardless of the inherent value of the material.

Part of this last question relates to the Neuro-Logical Levels we discussed earlier, as well as to good learning states. Think about it like this: If you haven't got a good place, or a good time, to learn something new, you won't. You'll be focused on those outside, environmental, concerns instead. This means that if the classroom, or other training setting isn't suitable, it becomes a distraction. If people are too busy, or can't get relief from their most important tasks, to attend a training session, they'll be thinking about those tasks rather than what is being presented. If they aren't as comfortable as possible, they'll be distracted. You can't order people to learn something new. You can make the opportunity comfortable, worthwhile, and as free from distractions as possible.

Once you've considered and taken care of the environmental issues, you then have to consider the specific behaviors you want people to be able to do. Good teachers and trainers use many modern methods to make learning enjoyable and easy, as much as possible. It is both an art and a science. This usually includes identifying specific activities that will help the people involved learn what they need to. But learning specific behaviors or tasks is not the same as learning a capability and the distinction is a very important one. For an easy example, think about learning to spell. Most of us learned to spell the word "Mississippi" by singing the letters out in sort of a chant. It's easy that way. But once someone's learned it, they've learned *only one specific behavior*: how to spell *Mississippi*. They haven't learned *how to spell* in general. That takes a whole different kind of learning. We don't learn to spell each word, one by one, in school even though it may have seemed that way. Actually, we learn a set of rules, how to visualize words, how to remember where we've seen them, and so forth. That is the *capability* of spelling and it's much more valuable than the *specific behavior* of spelling any single word.

This distinction is important in all training. If people only learn a set of operations, or disconnected procedures, without learning how and why those things work, they are handicapped from the start. They'll never be able to creatively solve problems, make judgments and decisions, or even know when they need help. Just as important to their learning is to really *believe* in their abilities to do these things. If a person doesn't believe they can do something, they usually won't even try. If they do try, it will probably be tentative and half-hearted, and we know what good that does. Beyond that, they have to identify themselves as capable, just as we discussed in the first section of this book. And they have to believe they are, and identify themselves as, important to the success of the team. Good training can help with all of these things. Bad training will leave people with one or more handicaps that are difficult to overcome.

So, training must be relevant and coordinated with other activities. It should address each of the Neuro-Logical Levels to be most effective. People should be in their best states to receive it. That means, if you are the one who needs some kind of special training, you can get yourself into the best state to learn–just as you have with other states. If it is someone else, maybe you can help them.

With this in mind, there are three ways you can do the next exercise, so read the instructions carefully first.

EXPERIMENT: DESIGNER STATE FOR TRAINING PROBLEMS

Step 1:

First decide how you wish to approach this; there are three options.

Option 1: If the current problem you are having is one involving training, think of a time when you had as similar a training related problem as you can remember – one that you handled well.

Option 2: If you, personally, are the one who needs some training, you might choose to think back on a time when you isolated your particular learning needs, located or developed a course of study, and got yourself into a really good state to learn (this could actually be *three different* states: one for isolating particular needs, one for developing or finding a course of study, and/or one for learning).

Option 3: If you believe someone else is in need of some training, think back to a time in which you were able to gently but persuasively convince this person, or someone else, to do so. Remember that this may take all your best interpersonal skills to accomplish, so you will want your most effective state for good communication (you may have developed this in the last exercise).

Again, imagine, that you can go back in time to the exact moment when you found or developed the solution to this problem, or got into the state of mind that you needed.

Jot down notes on the DESIGNER STATE WORK SHEET. On the Descriptive Label line, put the problem type or particular kind of state that this memory fits. On the Description of Content lines, put down the time you are remembering and whatever notes you need so that, later, when you look at this again, you will remember where it came from.

Step 2:
While you are remembering the feelings that go with this decision, change in viewpoint, or new understanding fill out the KINESTHETIC portion of the sheet.

Step 3:
Carefully examine whatever internal visual image, or images, you have while you're in this state. Fill out the VISUAL portion of the sheet now.

Step 4:
Now, again, listen to the sounds you have in your mind especially your own voice as you talk to yourself about this training problem you solved. You may remember specific conversations that occurred at that time. When you can clearly hear all that you need, fill out the AUDITORY portion of the sheet.

DESIGNER STATE WORK SHEET

Descriptive Label_____

Description of Content_____

_____

_____

VISUAL

Brightness	_____	Focus	_____
Distance	_____	Slide	_____
Size	_____	Motion Picture	_____
Shape	_____	Movement/Speed	_____
Location	_____	Associated	_____

Direction	_____	Disassociated	_____
Contrast	_____	Depth 3D/Flat	_____
Clarity	_____	Frame/No Frame	_____
Color	_____	Other?	_____

AUDITORY

Sounds	_____	Timbre	_____
Words	_____	Internal	_____
Location	_____	External	_____
Pitch	_____	Direction	_____
Tone	_____	Tempo	_____
Voice (Who?)	_____	Volume	_____
Distance	_____	Duration	_____
Rhythm	_____	Other?	_____

KINESTHETIC

Internal	_____	Proprioceptive	_____
External	_____	Shape	_____
Location	_____	Temperature	_____
Weight	_____	Movement	_____
Duration	_____	Intensity	_____
Size	_____	Moisture	_____
Pressure	_____	Texture	_____
Frequency	_____	Rhythm	_____
Tactile	_____	Balance	_____
Emotion?	_____	Other?	_____

OLFACTORY/GUSTATORY

Sweet	_____	Pungent	_____
Sour	_____	Intensity	_____
Salty	_____	Location	_____
Bitter	_____	Aromatic	_____
Specific taste	_____	Specific smell	_____

Description of Anchor_____

_____

Much of your experience of this last exercise surely depends on which of the options you chose. I broke it down into personal training problems, interpersonal ones and general ones. It makes sense if you think about it, but the most important thing is to be sure that whoever needs to get the training, gets it. People resist training for the obvious reasons of cost and time spent away from important tasks. These, of course, need to be carefully weighed to insure that the benefits are heavier than the costs–remember to think of this as a capital investment. In addition, many people in business have fears about the effects of training, the most common being that if people are trained too well, they'll leave to get better jobs. An old saying goes: "The only thing worse than having well trained people who leave, is having poorly trained ones who stay."

This is also an area in which expert help is a wise investment. Good training consultants will look at the specific needs for training, measured against the costs, and design a program or suggest alternatives accordingly. They will also assist in measuring the results and effectiveness of training on the people who receive it and the business as a whole. These consultants may be available inside your company, or outside. There arc also training organizations that often list specialized providers you may contact for help (American Society of Training & Development, National Society For Performance & Instruction, Society Of Human Resource Management, local university business departments). Take advantage of these if you feel your own experience, or the experience of the people around you, is lacking.

Systemic Problems
and
Environmental/Situational Problems

These can be closely related types of problems in several ways, and also closely related to training issues as well. First of all, they usually involve the need to see a larger picture than the previous problem types we've discussed, with the possible exception of some training problems. Second, they can seem the most insurmountable because they actually involve structures and patterns of relationships, not just individual ones. Third, in our education, we have been taught less about systems than just about anything else. As a result of this education, we suffer from *linear thinking*. That means we believe in direct cause and effect in most areas of our lives, especially problems. X + Y = Z, a linear equation, works fine for many simple problems. For more complex ones however, we need to understand how X, Y and Z *relate* to one another, in specific ways, that we can adjust and change. We may need to make a change that affects our whole alphabet.

How do we apply the concept of states to these kinds of problems?   For example, some of our problems relate to planning, productivity & limitations, or tools, materials, support, or the right time and space to function in. These aren't a matter of having a particular state to do well. But there have been times when we were *in* particular states and *did* them well. That may not make sense at first, but it will. The fact is, there have been times in all of our lives when we were faced with these very practical kinds of limitations. The kinds of things when clear foresight, logic, and an under-standing of what it is we were trying to do, was the most important thing to have. This kind of thinking can be impossible in the wrong state–but easy in the right one. Just as in the first option above, under training problems, if you can remember a time when you handled a similar kind of problem well, the state you handled that one in could be of great help handling a current one.

To begin with, remember that, if it is possible in the world, it is possible. It then just becomes a question of how. We have all heard people we know explain why their business is suffering. These most often involve personal or interpersonal problems. Most of us can recognize and focus on those readily, whether or not the solutions seem as obvious. But we absolutely *know* they can be solved. When people, however, say, "It's just the market (economy, competition, time of year, public attitudes, etc.) that is causing my problems," they sound different. Wise and knowing. Knowledgeable, to realize the broader issues at hand. Keenly insightful. Possessing a real perspective. A good feel for the pulse of the nation (market, economy, whatever). We all tend to act as if these kinds of things are beyond *everyone's* control. We throw up our hands and say something like, "Well maybe things will get better soon."

Think about the fallacy of this kind of thinking. And the danger. Remember if something is possible, it's possible. If *someone* is succeeding, you, they, and everyone else could too. Sure these kinds of problems can cause trouble. Sure they can be the most difficult to perceive, much less solve. But there are people who thrive on this sort of adversity. There are people who walk into seemingly impossible situations every day, and walk out successful and happy. They ask themselves, "How can I make this work?" rather than, "How could I have gotten myself into this?" They look toward possibilities rather than obstacles. They take a different view of the situation and see opportunities where others see insurmountable barriers.

The hopeful part of all this is that we have all overcome situations we couldn't figure out how to handle at first. Unfortunately, we tend to forget this at exactly the moment we need to *remember it. Clearly. Vividly. Thoroughly.*

These kinds of problems usually come down to taking a different view of what it is you're trying to do. Knowing the relationships between products and services, clients and their needs, delivery systems, economic considerations, competition (fair and unfair), and what is worthwhile doing, is crucial. Being able to look at each of these relationships, and clearly seeing the systems involved and how they interact with one another, leads to that understanding. Flexibility in perspective and viewpoint, which comes from altering your state, is what allows you to adapt to changes and understand these relationships in new ways when the need arises.

Taking the long view, for example, is something that comes naturally for some people and takes a little more work for others. We have all done it at one time or another in our lives. If you are in a position in business where this is necessary to your success, or for that matter your survival, having a state in which you can do so is invaluable. The same goes for all of the other states we talked about in Chapter 7, the ones that are universally useful. These are the kinds of states that come in handy when you have these more general kinds of problems. That's why I spent so much time describing them. You may want to look back over that list one more time, if you think that this problem you are currently working on is systemic or environmental/situational. The state you need might be right there waiting for you.

The following is an experiment you can use in several ways. You may want to repeat it if you think you need more than one state for handling your current problem, or if you would like to try it several ways.

EXPERIMENT: DESIGNER STATE FOR SYSTEMIC OR ENVIRONMENTAL/SITUATIONAL BUSINESS PROBLEMS

Step 1:

First decide how you wish to approach this; there are three options.

Option 1: If the current problem you are having is one of this type, think of a time when you had as similar a problem as you can remember–one that you handled well.

Option 2: If you believe you need one (or more–you can repeat this) of the states described in Chapter 7, go back to a time in your experience when you had that particular state.

Option 3: If you believe there is someone you know of, who you could model in the way we did earlier in this chapter, think of that person now. Then go back to that experiment, called "Borrowing Talent" and repeat the exercise with this current problem as your focus. You may use one of the DESIGNER STATE WORK SHEETS following this exercise, or one of the copies you made, if you already used that one.

If you chose Option 1 or 2, imagine that you can go back in time to the exact moment when you found or developed the solution to this problem, or got into the state of mind that you needed.

Jot down notes on the DESIGNER STATE WORK SHEET on the next page. On the Descriptive Label line, put the problem type or particular kind of state that this memory fits. On the Description of Content lines, put down the time you are remembering and whatever notes you need so that, later, when you look at this again, you will remember where it came from.

Step 2:

While you are remembering the feelings that go with this decision, change in viewpoint, or new understanding fill out the KINESTHETIC portion of the sheet.

Step 3:

Carefully examine whatever internal visual image, or images, you have while you're in this state. Fill out the VISUAL portion of the sheet now.

Step 4:

Now, again, listen to the sounds you have in your mind especially your own voice as you talk to yourself about this training problem you solved. You may remember specific conversations that occurred at that time. When you can clearly hear all that you need, fill out the AUDITORY portion of the sheet.

DESIGNER STATE WORK SHEET

Descriptive Label_____

Description of Content_____

_____

_____

VISUAL

Brightness	_____	Focus	_____
Distance	_____	Slide	_____
Size	_____	Motion Picture	_____
Shape	_____	Movement/Speed	_____
Location	_____	Associated	_____
Direction	_____	Disassociated	_____
Contrast	_____	Depth 3D/Flat	_____
Clarity	_____	Frame/No Frame	_____
Color	_____	Other?	_____

AUDITORY

Sounds	_____	Timbre	_____
Words	_____	Internal	_____
Location	_____	External	_____
Pitch	_____	Direction	_____
Tone	_____	Tempo	_____
Voice (Who?)	_____	Volume	_____
Distance	_____	Duration	_____
Rhythm	_____	Other?	_____

KINESTHETIC

Internal	_____	Proprioceptive	_____
External	_____	Shape	_____
Location	_____	Temperature	_____
Weight	_____	Movement	_____
Duration	_____	Intensity	_____
Size	_____	Moisture	_____
Pressure	_____	Texture	_____
Frequency	_____	Rhythm	_____
Tactile	_____	Balance	_____
Emotion?	_____	Other?	_____

OLFACTORY/GUSTATORY

Sweet	_____	Pungent	_____
Sour	_____	Intensity	_____
Salty	_____	Location	_____
Bitter	_____	Aromatic	_____
Specific taste	_____	Specific smell	_____

Description of Anchor_____

_____

I have taken you through a lot of experiments of basically the same form. This is because the more you do this, the more natural it becomes. The more natural it becomes, the more you will find yourself doing it *automatically* when you need to. The point is that it is an automatic process anyway. We all rely on our memories to help us retrieve past information, resources, ideas, and abilities. But we often hope that it will happen when we need it, rather than *doing it intentionally*. This problem solving model takes out the "hopefully" and puts in the "intentionally". That's really what people mean when they talk about taking charge of their own lives.

I also must remind you that there are lots of options to choosing which state of mind will work best for you. If you experiment, you will find your favorite methods for choosing and developing these states. Some people develop problem solving states that seem to work for them just about all the time. That's great if you can do it. Others practice modeling gifted people on a regular basis, and borrow their talent whenever they feel the need. It can work just as well. Still other people like to develop new states each time they need one, to improve flexibility.

Problem solving states are very valuable, and they are completely in your control. Each of the ones you've developed, through these exercises, has been designed with a specific purpose. Each has a DESIGNER STATE WORK SHEET filled out for it to jog your memory back to that state when you need it. The next step in the process is to show you how to get these states back quickly and easily, at the right times. Later we'll get into ways of enhancing the states, checking and refining the solutions, and carrying through to the well-formed outcomes you want and deserve.

Chapter 9

Controlling & Using States

Now it's time to learn to use your states for solving problems. This includes:

1. Getting into the state you need;
2. Staying in the state;
3. Developing solutions while you're in it; and
4. Saving the state for future use.

These processes are surprisingly simple. First, though, we need to understand a basic, naturally occurring process, called *anchoring*. It lies at the heart of all of these processes and makes them easy to use.

Retrieving states

Think about memory. I just spent three chapters asking you to use your memory in specific ways. Do you know exactly how you did it? When you recall some event or experience, how do you actually remember it? What causes the images and sounds in your head to come flooding back to you? What is the mechanism that causes you to react to something with a response, whether the response is an act, thought, or feeling? How do you know that, when you got a visual image, or some sounds in your mind, the feelings were really the ones that went with that particular memory? We generally take these psychological processes for granted, but that's "hopeful" not "intentional".

We have all had the experience of walking down the street, minding our own (or someone else's) business, and suddenly being struck with a memory. Sometimes the blow is a severe one, sometimes not. Often, if we pay attention to our surroundings, we can identify some object, sound, or smell that seems to be the cause of our sudden recall. It could be almost anything. A stranger's facial expression, or even posture, can remind us of someone we know. We then have a memory that involved that person, and suddenly the images, sounds, and feelings that go with it. It is as if we are not in our present surroundings any longer, but rather hurled back in time to that former, perhaps forgotten, place. We are with that person again in our own minds, and we have the experiences that go along with that former place and time.

Familiar? Of course. Specific memories, and the things that trigger them, are what make us unique individuals. But it is the content of these memories, and the specific things that trigger them, that are unique to each of us. The *process* by which the triggering mechanism works is not. That particular facial expression, song, or scent may only affect you. And certainly the memory you have is all yours. But we are *all* affected by *some* facial expression, song, or scent, at some time. That experience is universal among fully functioning people.

This basic sort of relationship can be observed in just about all animals, occasionally even ones as simple as single-celled bacteria. In human beings, though, it is much more dramatic. Moreover, because of our greater complexity of experience, we are able to use this naturally occurring process to achieve our goals and make life more interesting.

Given that we all know what it's like to have one of those memories appear suddenly and spontaneously, wouldn't it be nice to be able to have *any* memory of our choosing, *whenever* we want it? Unfortunately, most of us are victimized by this mechanism, rather than benefited by it. We have a sad or upsetting memory, and feel as if our minds are playing nasty tricks on us. We have a problem and feel helpless, rather than immediately remembering times we've solved similar problems effectively and creatively. We forget that our brains simply do what we, and others, have taught them to do. The good news is we can just as effectively re-train our brains to do more useful things instead. This means, instead of getting into problem states and staying stuck in them, we can get into the states for solving them right away.

This process may seem mysterious at first, but it is really quite simple. Anything that is so universally known usually has a fairly simple explanation in terms of experience. The person who explained it most thoroughly at first was Pavlov, well over a hundred years ago. In his study of reflexes in animals, he focused on dogs and their response to the sight of food. Everyone who has a dog knows that a dog will begin to drool when you bring out the supper dish (I do the same when I see a pizza). This is called the salivary response. It's normal and seems to occur in most animals with similar digestive systems. This physiological response helps the dog (and us) begin the digestion process. Pavlov wanted to know if he could exert some *influence* on this naturally occurring process and bring it under the control of some outside agent, i.e. him.

He decided to add something to the conditions of the dog seeing the food. Each time he showed the food to the dog, he rang a bell. He did this a number of times, so that the dog would "associate" the food and the bell with one another. Then he began to *only* ring the bell for the dog, without showing it the food. Sure enough, the dog would begin to drool just as he had originally, but this time with no food in sight. Each time the dog heard the bell, he would salivate. This continued for a while and then gradually wore off, since, somehow the dog "knew" that the bell, after a while, no longer had anything to do with the appearance of food (in other words, the dog learned to re-associate the sound of the bell with *no* food).

Pavlov called this entire process conditioning, since it was built on setting up specific conditions to create it. This was the basis of stimulus-response psychology. The showing of food to the dog was the unconditional (natural) stimulus to which the dog responded with salivation. The ringing of the bell was the conditioned (created) stimulus to which the dog was "trained" to respond.

The most important part is that when the unconditional stimulus (the food) was "paired" with the conditioned stimulus (the sound of the bell), the dog actually *changed* in some way. We don't really know what the dog was thinking (or even if dogs "think" in the way we normally imagine it). We do know the dog changed. In very real terms, he "learned" to respond, physically, to a previously unimportant event: the ringing of a bell.

This also explains the triggering mechanism we have been talking about in *us*. That facial expression that brings back our powerful memory is just like Pavlov's bell. It is a conditioned stimulus, a signal that causes a response in us. Many people believe that most of our responses to anything have been conditioned in the same sense that Pavlov conditioned his dogs. Whether or not it is actually true is irrelevant. Once we become aware of the process, and how it works in us, we can begin to exert the kind of influence over ourselves that Pavlov exerted over the dogs; in other words, use it. We have a decided advantage, however. We can simply use our imaginations to present ourselves with a stimulus. For example, we can imagine the last time we had our favorite dish, in our favorite restaurant, and voila! salivation.

Figure 9.i

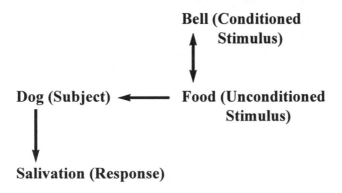

PAVLOVIAN CONDITIONING

Figure 9.ii

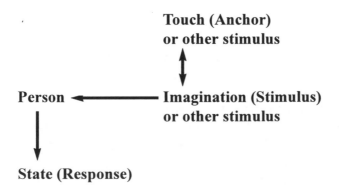

ANCHORING

The same process can be used for lots of other, less glandular, responses of course. For example, when I asked you to remember a time you were able to solve a particular problem, how did you do it? Probably you did some sort of search through your memory for an experience that you had mentally filed away in the "problem file", whatever that means. More specifically, did you sort through a series of internal visual images until you had a feeling of being stuck in a problem? Did these images look, literally, like a series of snapshots? Did they look more like a movie? Or perhaps, did you simply say the word "stuck" or "problem" to yourself, and then feel it? Which sense and which sub-modalities are crucial for you when you remember some particular experience? Do the following experiment.

EXPERIMENT: TRIGGERING MEMORY

Step 1:
Remember the designer state you developed in the last chapter specifically for solving the type of problem you have now. You may have come up with several states appropriate for this problem, so just choose one for now. Look at the DESIGNER STATE WORK SHEET you made up for that one.

Step 2:
Allow yourself, briefly, to go fully into the state again by remembering the original experience that created it. Again, notice the visual images, sounds and feelings that go with this state. Use the DESIGNER STATE WORK SHEET to remind you of the specifics if that helps–that's what it's for.

Step 3:
When you have experienced this state again for a few moments, get up and walk around for a minute or two. This is to get you back into your normal state, *out of the designer state*. This is called "breaking the state."

Step 4:
Now sit back down and recreate only the visual image from the designer state. Then make sure to adjust the sub-modalities so that they are just like the descriptions on the DESIGNER STATE WORK SHEET.

Notice if the entire state comes back, with all of the sounds and feelings that go with it.

If so, get up and walk around for a minute or two, again to get back into your normal state, *(breaking) out of the designer state.*

Step 5:

Now sit back down and recreate only the auditory portion from the designer state: the sounds. Then, again, make sure to adjust the sub-modalities so that they are just like the descriptions on the DESIGNER STATE WORK SHEET.

Notice if the entire state comes back this time, along with all of the visual images and feelings that are a natural part of it.

If so, get up and walk around for a minute or two, again, to get back into your normal state – *break out of the designer state.*

This is a basic awareness experiment to determine what "stimulates" you to this state. Ask yourself, now, how you got into the state earlier. In other words, if just before you got into the state you made the visual image, *that's* the trigger, or stimulus, for that response. The same could be true of the sounds. Each of these is a part of the experience of that state, so perhaps just calling up one part brings on the entire experience. Often this is the case.

In NLP we call that stimulus a *naturally occurring anchor.* It's the same thing as an unconditional stimulus. It can be almost anything, as long as it works. For some people it will be a visual image, for others a sound, or another feeling. Some people even get a particular taste in their mouths or a smell just prior to the response. The important thing is to determine what is a working, already occurring, anchor for this state. You may even have several.

When you have determined your natural anchor for this state, practice it a few times. Often, an anchor becomes stronger with use, especially when there is some payoff for it. That is the reason to use this designer state for solving personal problems to begin with. We have anchors, already existing, for just about every imaginable experience there is. Some we want, like the ones that produced our designer states. Others we don't, like the ones that keep us stuck in problem states.

Anchors are extremely powerful tools. They are only tools, however, when *you are controlling them* rather than the other way around. Your naturally occurring anchors were created the same way as the natural salivary response in the dog. The dog learned as it was growing to salivate at the sight of food. So every time it saw food it would salivate as one of the first steps in the digestive process. By the same token, your naturally occurring anchors were created because you learned to associate certain images, sounds, thoughts, and feelings together with that past experience. In a sense they were all a part of the original experience that they now recreate. The fact that they were accidental makes them no less influential. They work. The dog, however, wouldn't dream of using this process intentionally to help his digestion. Come to think of it, he probably doesn't dream about anything in the future. Until now, you probably wouldn't have thought of using these images, or sounds, to get back these states either. But you *could* have.

You could also create, artificially, other anchors to get you into these problem solving states, or any others of your choosing. For the dog, the bell became an anchor, artificially created, but effective nonetheless. It is much simpler for us. The first step is to practice creating anchors in yourself, at will. Remember that an anchor can be almost anything. I say that because, without you realizing it, we already created some artificial anchors for those designer states in the last chapter. Remember those sheets, with the MEMORY line at the top?

EXPERIMENT: WRITTEN ANCHORS

Step 1:
Choose any of the designer states you'd like to have back right now.

Step 2:
Go back to the DESIGNER STATE WORK SHEET you filled out on that state, with the brief description and all the visual, auditory, and kinesthetic sub-modalities.

Step 3:
Read the MEMORY line description you wrote.

Step 4:

Now pay attention to the memory of that experience as it floods back into your consciousness now. Check through the sub-modalities and see if what you have written matches your experience from just reading that top line.

Reading it out loud, or at least hearing the words in your mind, may make it even more real for you. If any of the sub-modalities don't match, or the experience doesn't seem as real for you as it did before, change each sub-modality until it is exactly the way it was originally. That is the reason you made these notes to yourself.

I trust you now know why I spent so much time, and took so much care, to be sure you understood how to use the DESIGNER STATE WORK SHEETS. They have become anchors for these states for solving problems. You can turn to them, whenever you need to, for help with the specific kinds of problems each was designed for. I want to take this concept of anchoring even further for you, however. You can easily create anchors to be used any time you want, even without the sheets you filled out. (Also, you can do this for any kind of state you think would be worthwhile having, not just ones for solving problems.)

Anchors can be in any of the five senses: sight, sound, feeling, taste, or smell. They can be on the outside of us, or in our minds. We've been concentrating so far on internal visual and auditory ones only because it was convenient for the procedures I wanted to present. In fact, in NLP, we generally begin teaching people to anchor themselves by using the sense of touch. A touch is specific enough to be able to duplicate exactly, and is therefore easiest. Do the following experiment.

EXPERIMENT: TOUCH ANCHORS

Step 1:

Begin by going back to this same designer state by using your DESIGNER STATE WORK SHEET, just as you did before.

Step 2:

When you are fully in this very useful state, press the tips of your thumb and forefinger together, on your left hand. Do this with gentle but firm pressure.

Literally, I'm asking you to "pair" and "associate" this touch with this state. Provided that you do this as I've described, this touch will become as much a part of the experience of this state (an anchor) as the visual image, sounds and feelings.

Step 3:

Next, get up and walk around for a minute. This is to get you back to your more or less neutral, or normal, state, just as before.

Step 4:

Now sit back down and immediately press your thumb and forefinger together, exactly as before. Make sure to use the same touch, pressure, etc.

Step 5:

Pay attention to your feelings and the images and sounds in your mind. Does the state come back, fully and realistically? Probably, to some extent, it does. This is how you test an anchor to see if it works.

Step 6:

Repeat this entire process several times until this designer state is just as strong, from simply "firing the anchor" (touching your thumb and forefinger together) as it was from your original memory and from using the sheet to read from. Remember, the more vivid and "real" the experience seems on the inside, the easier it will be to anchor.

Step 7:

Now fill in the line at the bottom of the page marked Description of Anchor. Put down: "touch thumb and forefinger together on left hand" or whatever you need to remember exactly how to do it again. You'll need to know later.

The importance of duplicating the touch exactly needs to be stressed. When Pavlov had conditioned the dogs to the bell, he added another experiment to his study of the phenomenon. He tried using bells of various pitches and tones to determine whether the dogs would respond to any bell, or only the one he had paired with the food. There was a direct relationship between how close the bell sounded to the original and how strong the salivary response was. For example, a bell a few notes higher or lower produced a slightly weakened response in the dogs. One several octaves higher or lower produced little or no response. In NLP we have done these anchoring experiments with many thousands of people in a variety of settings. It seems that the location and pressure used in a physical touch anchor *can* be very crucial in some people. Even a slight variation, in some people, is enough to reduce the effectiveness of the anchor considerably.

Another point to make is that any touch you choose to use as an anchor should be one you don't normally use. If you happen to spend a lot of time touching your thumb and forefinger together, choose some other kind of touch, perhaps another finger and your thumb, as your anchor. The reason for this should be fairly obvious. If Pavlov tried to associate the food and the bell in a dog that lived in a bell factory, how would the dog make the connection? Bells would be associated with everything, and, therefore, nothing.

Also, it turns out that this associative process is an *unconscious* one. It happens at some neurological level, in human beings, that is more "primitive" than our usual conscious reasoning. This makes intuitive sense in the light of this process's effectiveness with extremely primitive beasts. In fact, some of the animals that psychologists have successfully conditioned–roaches, worms, and bacteria–have no neurological equipment, as we think of it, at all.

If all this sounds a bit too mechanical, I apologize. Often when people first learn these concepts they remark that they don't much appreciate being compared with creatures they usually avoid, spray, or step on. I don't like it either. But that has little to do with the effectiveness of the techniques. They work, plain and simple. Pavlovian, or Classical, conditioning is a fact of life. It works, at least in some ways, in the same way in people as in other organisms. Our uniqueness as a species comes from our richness of experience, and therefore from our ability to control the process rather than be controlled by it. It also seems that mechanistic structures like this are extremely useful for the purposes of teaching and learning *procedures*. As you practice and learn more about how this works in your personal experience, you can add in your own stylistic adaptations.

Enhancing states

I must also point out that, although this technique works primarily on an unconscious level, you don't need to be "unconscious" when you use it. Another feature of human beings is the unique interaction between our unconscious processes and our conscious ones. This is the whole basis of NLP, and indeed of all approaches to controlling human behavior. It's certainly the major difference between us and the other beasts I mentioned earlier. We can consciously combine anchors of various types to produce enhanced effects. These can take the form of self-hypnotic suggestions added to our anchors. In this way we can make our anchors, such as the one you now have, for one of your designer states, even more powerful and useful. Without explaining the processes by which these kinds of suggestions work and are used, I'll give you some. A good start would be creating one to go along with the anchor you just created.

EXPERIMENT: VERBAL ANCHORS

Step 1:
Fire the anchor for your first designer state, i.e. touch your thumb and forefinger together as before, and at the same time say to yourself: "When I touch my thumb and finger this way, I will fully remember (that earlier time) when I was able to solve a personal problem." This is a well formed hypnotic suggestion for you, and one we've found particularly effective in this case. It doesn't matter if you say it out loud or not. Again, the suggestion will become a part of the experience. If you want to, you can substitute the description of the state that you wrote on the MEMORY line for "that earlier time."

Step 2:

Break this state–get up and walk around until you are back in your normal state.

Step 3:

Now fire the anchor and say the sentence again. Does the response come back stronger than before?

Step 4:

Write down the sentence, exactly as you said it, on your DESIGNER STATE WORK SHEET, if you need to. If you put it down next to the description of your anchor, it may serve to remind you best.

It turns out, as well, that combining anchors will often create an additive effect on their strength. For example, if you have two separate anchors for the same feeling, and fire them at the same time, you will often create an intensified experience of that feeling, one stronger than either of the individual anchors would have produced by itself. I use the word "often" in this case because there are conditions. You must be sure of just what you are anchoring to use this tool effectively. Sometimes when people are first learning, they are a bit too cavalier about the procedure. They often end up anchoring several other things besides what they expected to, or were aware of. This can produce bizarre results.

When I began teaching this process, I had a number of experiences in workshops of the following phenomenon. I'd instruct a group of people in the anchoring process, just as I've done with you. I'd ask them to go back in their minds to a time when they felt pleasant and relaxed. Then I'd watch them close their eyes, lean back for a moment, then burst into tears. The first few times this happened I had to scratch my head, and then ask a few questions.

I found that everyone who reacted in this way did one of two things. Often they would just go back to a memory that was really painful, rather than pleasant. Wrong memory. Simple enough. They just needed another memory to go back to. The second possibility was that they would indeed go back to the memory that was most pleasant and relaxing for them. Then they would comment to themselves about how they could *never* have things that good again. That is a pretty depressing thought. So depressing, in fact, that it worked to overwhelm them immediately with feeling depressed rather than feeling pleasant and relaxed. Same solution: a different memory was needed (there are other ways to handle this situation, but we needn't go into them here).

EXTERNALIZATION

One problem people often have, especially when trying to solve a thorny problem, is that they get overwhelmed inside. They feel out of control because there is too much, often unclear or conflicting, information to deal with. And the information, and choices, frustrations and fears, seem to be swimming around in a giant soup of confusion.

A good way to handle this is to *externalize* all of this internal confusion. That means getting it out of our minds where it is causing more harm than good. There are a number of ways of doing this. Think about all those detective stories we've seen on TV or in the movies. Some clever cop or group of investigators chart out how the crime was committed on a blackboard. Or they put the pictures up on a wall with notes all over the place that explain what happened. Sometimes we'll see one making notes on a page linking different ideas together in some form. These are examples of externalizing all of the information so that it can be *controlled and organized.*

There is no wrong way to do this. Anything that helps get all of the "data" out of our heads and onto paper (or whatever) can help us get some handle on it. Some people like "mind maps" that place some central concept in the center of a page, surrounded by related pieces spreading out, like branches, filling up the page. Others (like me) prefer simple series of lists of everything relevant, on the computer screen, in plain sight. Some like note cards they can organize and re-organize until they can make sense out of them. There are even those who prefer just talking into a tape recorder. Sometimes hearing their own voices talking about the problem seems to take it outside of themselves and provide a new perspective.

Another method, developed by Disney and employed regularly in the movie industry, is the "story board." In this case you would actually draw pictures representing each "scene" and arrange them in some logical order. It's extremely useful in identifying missing pieces in a scenario. This can be helpful in problem solving since sometimes we are missing some not-so-obvious piece of the puzzle. Having an external image, or series of images, can help.

The point to all of these is to relieve the internal stress caused by information overload. Any time we can do that it will help us get into a better state for creatively solving problems. It might even provide clear solutions by giving us control of all the crucial information.

Each of these is an example of a class of responses called polarity responses. Effectively, a polarity response gives you the polar opposite of what you are looking for. We have all had the experience of dealing with people who do exactly the opposite of everything we ask them. Two-year-olds are experts at this. And people who don't learn to change, after they're finished being two, often have problems relating to others later in life. Successful ones occasionally become entrepreneurs. The rest go to work in positions where they can drive the rest of us crazy (or make us develop new designer states for handling difficult people). In reality, of course, we all polarity respond to lots of things. Rightfully so. The key is being conscious of how, and under what circumstances, we respond to input and then making wise choices.

Most important for our interests here, however, is that you be aware of your feelings and other responses as you set up your anchor for these designer states. I've encountered people who have two anchors that they *believe* create the same feeling in them, but they haven't paid close attention. What they have really done is anchored two very different kinds of states. They then fire the anchors simultaneously, hoping for a stronger effect. What they actually get is some other response altogether. It is a combination of the two anchored responses. If they are the opposite of one another, as in the polarity response combined with the desired response, the outcome is usually nothing – they cancel each other out.

To be sure that you are combining similar anchors, check the sub-modalities. If you want to combine several problem solving states together, as I've suggested, make sure that the sub-modalities are as close to one another as possible. In other words, if the first visual image is very bright, large, and clear, make sure the other one is too. The same with the sounds and feelings.

Another way to enhance these states should already be evident. You can carefully adjust the sub-modalities so that the experience is more powerful or real for you. It may be that intensifying the feeling makes it easier for you to come up with creative new solutions to the type of problem you wish to solve. If that is the case, try brightening the image and making it a bit larger. Or try turning up the volume or clarity of the voices in your mind. That may give you the intensity of feeling you want. I suggest, however, that you try one sub-modality at a time, adjusting it slowly and carefully. Sometimes changing several at once simply causes a feeling of confusion, or an image that seems unreal, or weird. That may not help you much.

Hopefully you are already wondering how many different ways you can use this phenomenon to help yourself. The number is almost limitless. If you use your imagination you can find lots of things you could change, and states you could use, that would make your life more fruitful and enjoyable.

Here is a useful list of guidelines to help you use anchoring more effectively, some of which we've already mentioned:

1. Make each anchor *distinct* from anything else you normally do or it will be contaminated by ("collapsed with") all the other states you go into when you fire the anchor. In other words, if you hold your thumb and forefinger together, as a habit, on a regular basis, use something else for the anchor you want. Otherwise, you'll be firing it all the time and it will slowly "dilute" itself to nothing.

2. Make sure you are *really in the state* you want anchored, not just thinking about what it should be like. You will anchor whatever state you are in when you set up the anchor–for better or worse – the anchor doesn't care which.

3. Anchors should be *tested* for effectiveness when they are set. Make sure you anchored what you want to have, in yourself (or in others), by first breaking the state, then firing the anchor to insure that the resource state returns. The reason it is important to break the state first is that, if you are already in it, you won't know if the anchor really produces it at will.

4. It may take several tries to get the anchor to work. This is especially true when you are first learning since you may have to practice duplicating placement and timing. Be patient, and give yourself a reasonable number of attempts. Also, if you have trouble with one kind of anchor (touch, words, etc.) choose another.

5. Anchors can be "stacked" meaning they combine in strength and quality, by setting the same anchor for several *similar* useful states. (Anchors can also be

187

"collapsed" on each other, effectively canceling each other out; a method for getting rid of unwanted anchors. (This is beyond the scope of this book, so check the bibliography for more information.)

6. Anchors can work in any representational system (sensory modality). Practice using touch, hand and facial gestures, and voice tones and inflections. Anchors are all around us, and inside of our thinking processes. They cannot be avoided but they can be controlled. Remember: ANCHORS WORK! So use them wisely.

7. The more internal awareness and sensory acuity you have, the easier it will be to insure success. You'll know if you are in the desired state or not. And the more external awareness and sensory acuity the better in working with others. (Again, beyond the scope of this book).

Developing solutions with anchors

Now that you can get into your designer state(s) for solving the problem you're working on, the rest is even easier. You will simply use the anchor(s) you set up for getting into this state(s) and develop solutions while you are in that resourceful state(s), if you haven't already. Remember, what prevents us from solving many of our problems is that we are in a "stuck" state, separated from the resources we have, to be creative and solve the problem. The anchor(s) is your key to unlocking that stuck state and getting out of it and into a more productive one.

EXPERIMENT: USING YOUR ANCHOR TO DEVELOP SOLUTIONS

Step 1:
Fire your anchor for the designer state you have developed that you know will help you solve the problem you are working on. This means touch your thumb and forefinger together, if that is the anchor. Also, say any words to yourself that you use to enhance the state.

Step 2:
Check your DESIGNER STATE WORK SHEET to be sure that you are fully in the state. Make whatever adjustments to the visual image and the sounds you need to insure that the feeling is the one you want–nice and strong.

Step 3:
Go back to the outcome you decided on for this problem. Check your notes from earlier in the book if you need to.

Step 4:
Hold the anchor to help you maintain the state while you do the following.
Think about the problem. Think about the outcome you want, that you developed earlier. Look at your notes on this to refresh your memory and help you focus on what you want.

Step 5:
Imagine what you might do about solving this problem and getting this outcome, while you are in this powerfully resourceful state.

Step 6:
Remember a previous experience of this problem. *While in this more resourceful state*, allow yourself to go back through the memory and imagine handling the situation or problem in a different way. Allow new solutions, new ideas, powerful resources and abilities to *flow naturally* through your mind. Watch and listen inside for new ways of dealing with the problem or situation you had at that time. Feel the strength of these anchors as these new ideas and possible ways you could have handled the problem come to you.
Repeat this with several past instances of the problem situation.
Write down these new ideas, to jog your memory later, if you can do so without disrupting this resourceful state (you can always fire the anchor again if you need to). Make a list of your intended solution(s).

This exercise is the culmination of all that time you spent carefully defining the problem space, matching your problem to a specific type, and learning to control your state of mind. It may be worthwhile to repeat this last procedure though in my experience, if you followed instructions *and gave yourself enough time in the state*, the chances are that the solutions you came up with will be very effective and natural. In the next section of the book you'll go through some exercises to help you insure this and to "test" your solutions.

Anchors in everyday life

Before finishing with this subject, though, I want to describe several other ways for you to think about this important process in your life.

Anchors are everywhere. Throughout your day you encounter hundreds, at least. Simply getting up in the morning will send you through a number of routines that start your day. Many of us shower, dress, breakfast and engage in other activities in routine sorts of ways. Each step in the routine is an anchor for the next. It's what makes the sequence continue. Spend some time exploring your own routines of daily living. You may discover some interesting and useful things about yourself.

In addition, anchors can, certainly, be outside of us. I mentioned other people's facial expressions, voice tones, and postures already. But objects apply as well. Many people surround themselves with good luck charms or other things in every place they go. If you think about it you'll realize that these are nothing more than reminders of certain experiences. A picture of a loved one on a desk usually gives us some of the feelings we have toward that person. Pictures, in fact, are one of the best examples of anchors in our daily lives.

Beyond people and things, though, surroundings themselves become extremely powerful anchors. Intuitively, most of us know this. When we walk into a room we have not been in for some time, most of us find ourselves remembering past experiences in that place. Then we often have the feeling that went with a powerful experience we had there, or maybe just the last time we were there. One reason these kinds of anchors are so important is that they can be the most limiting. Sometimes when a person has had a "bad" experience in some place, they have a hard time going there again.

This often happens to people in their workplace. They have something happen to them that they can't seem to shake off. Then work becomes difficult. This can be the source of situational problems in business as well as in our personal lives.

But, by the same token, good experiences in the workplace, or anywhere for that matter, can make us look forward to going there again. They can also be a constant reminder of the kinds of things and experiences we want in life. They can make work, school, or life itself a real joy. Wouldn't it be nice to have our surroundings anchor our states for effective problem solving? Use and care for your anchors where you need them and this will actually happen.

That is how life works. People who are unhappy all the time have lots of effective anchors to remind them to be that way. Often they are strong enough anchors to overpower any wayward pleasantness that may crop up. The reverse is true for people who seem to be happy all the time. You see, the brain doesn't make judgments on the value of an anchor. It doesn't care whether the experience is nice or not. It just responds. It is up to us to consciously decide which ones we want and don't want. Then it is up to us to use what we know to get the ones we want and remove the rest.

If you ask elderly people to tell you about their memories, it will give you a big clue about their demeanor. Elderly people who seem content and happy generally remember the good times they have had. Those who seem unhappy and are full of complaints will often swear to you that nothing good has ever happened to them. We all know it isn't true. It's just what they remember, because of the state that they're in. Memories are anchors and anchors trigger other similar memories. You might want to start planning now. A future is a terrible thing to waste.

Finally, each word in our language is an anchor for some experience. That is the reason words mean such different things to different people. The words aren't different, only each person's individual understanding of them. Very few people are prompted to think of a dictionary definition for each word they hear. A word brings up an image; a vision, sound, or feeling. These are based on our experience of that word throughout our lives. A good communicator knows how to use words to create certain powerfully meaningful responses in others.

My final suggestion for you is to spend time truly exploring this phenomenon in your life and work. The next time you hear "that special song" (as in "they're playing our song"), try to remember how it became special. The same goes for that old movie on TV that brings back memories. An old book, car, or friend. Spend time, as well, paying attention to your responses to new things. Do they trigger memories of other experiences? How about the mundane routine things in your life? How did they get that way? Do you want to change them? You have only to begin. Remember, though, that's only a suggestion.

Chapter 10

Building A Compelling Future

Fine-tuning solutions

Developing solutions to problems, or even ways to meet goals, is *not* the last step in the process. In fact, at this point, even if you believe the solutions you have developed are great, there is much more you can do to insure that you actually carry out your plan with enthusiasm, consistency, and awareness. This is where we look back to where we have come from, before we go forward.

Let's go back to the first part of the book–the part where we carefully figured out what we wanted in the first place. For example, the sections on self, purpose and audience were designed to help you answer the most important questions about your role, the role of others, and what you really wanted. This needs to be carried all the way through this project (not to mention life). And if you have specific questions to ask while you carry out your plan, at specific times, you'll insure that you don't create more problems than you are solving.

The first question is, "Will the solution actually work to accomplish this goal–will I get the outcome?" To answer it, look back to Chapter 2 and the well formed outcome you wrote–this was your FINAL SHORT TERM OUTCOME. Then do the following experiment:

EXPERIMENT: TESTING SOLUTIONS – YOUR POSITION

Step 1:
Write your well formed outcome on the lines below, or on a separate piece of paper, to help you keep in mind what it is that you want.

FINAL SHORT TERM OUTCOME:_____

_____

Step 2:

Now look back at your intended solution(s) to the problem or situation you are working on. These are the ones from the last experiment in Chapter 9: USING YOUR ANCHOR TO DEVELOP SOLUTIONS. Have the notes or list you made handy and take a look at them now to have in mind, along with your intended outcome.

Note: You may want to close your eyes to do the following thoroughly, so read the instructions first before going on.

Step 3:

Imagine going into the future now, and carrying out the solution (or the first action on your list). Carry through to a point in the action past the actual finish of your plan, so that you can see the results. You are directing your own movie here, and you are the main character.

Remember that you need to imagine that you are actually doing these things, so the image is associated. Make it as real as you possibly can, adjusting any sub-modalities of the sights, sounds and feelings you need to so that it seems as though you are in the process of solving the problem *now*. This should seem just as vivid as the memories you explored earlier to develop your anchors–as much like reality as possible.

Listen to how you and others around you sound. Watch how the action looks. Feel how you feel.

Step 4:

Pay attention to whether you get the outcome, as you had imagined you would when you developed this solution, or set of actions. Does it work?

Step 5:

Pay attention to how this *feels* as you go through it. It should be a great feeling, compelling, interesting and exciting. Those are some of the feelings that go along with solving a problem or reaching a goal. In some cases, a sense of relief might be appropriate as well.

Step 6:

If this feels just as you would like it to, and the actions you're taking actually seem to work to get the outcome, that's what you're looking for. If not, it's OK, you'll get there soon.

Step 7:

Now take a few moments to come back into the room you're actually in, reorient yourself to your present time and place, and feel comfortable and alert.

There is obviously no perfect way to feel about something. Some feelings are useful, some aren't. I would prefer that you feel good while you go through this process, but more important, I want you to feel *compelled to go all the way* to the completion of your outcome, even if only in your imagination. Hopefully, you imagined yourself going all the way to the conclusion of your problem, with a great solution, fully complete, with great results and great feelings. If what you found instead were unpleasant feelings, no problem: we'll fix it.

Ask yourself about your *role* in this again. Is it still compatible with the solution you have developed? If not, it could cause you some confusion. This could be the source of discomfort if there is any. You could look over the same questions you answered back in Chapter 1 about your role in this situation. They are just as appropriate here. With the solution you have developed firmly in mind, along with the feelings you generated in yourself as you imagined carrying out your plan, again ask yourself these questions:

1. Am I sure of who I am as a person, and how this affects me in my work?
2. What role am I playing in this problem, or in taking on the responsibility of solving this problem? Is it my usual "normal" role in my job, or outside of my normal role?
3. Have I, perhaps, taken on more than one role? If so, are these various roles compatible with one another?
4. Are any of my roles competing with one another (i.e. am I competing with myself)? Am I competing with someone else?

5. Have I chosen a role that will make my work more difficult by its very nature?
6. Is there a particular tone, or attitude that goes with this role I've chosen? Is it one I really want–i.e. does it fit with who I am as a person?

Another good place to look again, also, is at our basic presuppositions, and values, and ask ourselves if the solutions we have come up with follow naturally from those foundations. It might be a good idea to look back at Chapter 2 now, to refresh your memory. Take a look again at the two lists you made called: **Adjusted *Personal* Values** and **Adjusted *Business* Values**. Write them down again here, or at least have them handy.

Adjusted *Personal* Values	Adjusted *Business* Values
1._____	1._____
2._____	2._____
3._____	3._____
4._____	4._____
5._____	5._____
6._____	6._____
7._____	7._____
8._____	8._____
9._____	9._____
10._____	10._____

Ask yourself, now as you look these over, if there is any conflict between the *solutions* you have come up with and either of these lists of values. If there are, they could certainly cause uncomfortable feelings and a lack of drive toward completing your outcome. With this in mind, do you need to make any changes in the way you would carry out your solution(s) so that they would be more compatible with your values?

Once you have imagined how you will solve this problem, and insured that you maintain the integrity of your personal identity, you need to do the same for the other people involved. Your solution needs to work for them, as well as for you. Since you need their help and support, naturally you want to give it to them too.

The questions you want to ask yourself here are as important as those we have just gone over. Though you asked yourself a number of things about the other people involved much earlier in the process, it's helpful to do it again, now that you have a solution in mind. The specific actions you take now will involve, affect, and require the cooperation of these other important people around you. Have the following questions in mind, and then go on to the next experiment which will help you answer them (it might be helpful to look over Chapter 3 again, and the answers you gave then):

1. Who else is involved in this situation, and therefore the solution you have come up with? What kind of contribution do each of them make in this respect?
2. How is the system itself involved, or affected? How will this affect how you carry out your solution?
3. How have you communicated with others who are involved or affected? Have you maintained and considered the effects on these important relationships?
4. Have you considered the individual needs of each person involved?
5. Have you considered the individual characteristics (meta-programs), working styles, and tendencies of each of the other people involved?

To fully answer these questions, or even to predict likely answers, it is important to imagine each person's specific role in your proposed solution. There are a number of ways to do this. First, though, another look at one of the processes we touched on earlier is in order.

People often stress the need to be *objective* in a variety of areas, problem solving among them. NLP is the study of *subjectivity*, what happens inside of us, in our internal thoughts and feelings. But it teaches us how to be objective as well; to see ourselves from the outside as others would. I want to introduce you to a procedure for objectivity–one that is quite useful in a variety of ways. As you may have guessed, it involves visual disassociation as we discussed earlier. We have all done this at one time or another.

First, an eye-opening example. Some years ago, I was conducting a seminar for people who were very afraid of certain social situations, especially meeting new people and dating. I used this procedure for becoming objective–which also happens to eliminate fear and other unwanted emotions–and the results were remarkable. The participants in the seminar were all more than pleasantly surprised. After the evening was over, one of the men in the seminar came up and asked me a question I never expected: "Were you ever involved in military counter-espionage work?" The rather surprised answer of "NO!" was quickly followed by "But why do you ask?" The man said that he had been a spy, working in counter-espionage during the Korean War. Part of his training had been almost exactly the same technique that I had just taught him in the seminar.

It worked like this. During the war, this man had been systematically trained that whenever he was in trouble, trapped, or in danger of being discovered, he was to imagine that he could float up in the air above the situation, look down on himself and the other people involved, from an objective "third-person" point of view. Then he was to pretend he was playing with the pieces in a chess game. Each person involved, including himself, was to be thought of as simply a piece to be played, cleverly and boldly. Of course he could only move himself first, but this would suggest how all the other pieces should be moved in response. He finished his story with "It saved my life six times!"

I then asked, "Since you know how to do this powerful technique already, why haven't you been using it in your personal life?" The response: "Never thought of it." In fact, he had forgotten all about it since his life was no longer in danger! I then suggested that, "you could think, now, about other things you have learned in your life that might be applied to making yourself a better person." The man walked off, slightly sheepish, but extremely thoughtful.

This is a visualization technique that produces very different sets of perceptions, feelings, and actually, a different state of consciousness (as you already know). Here's an experiment.

EXPERIMENT: ASSOCIATION & DISASSOCIATION

Step 1:

Imagine, as vividly as possible, that you are now walking onto a beach at an ocean or large lake. It is a hot day and you can feel the heat of the sun on your back and the heat of the sand on your bare feet. You can see the water stretching out into the distance in front of you and the beach to your right and your left. There are sea gulls, other people, and the normal beach sights. You can hear the waves, along with the laughter of children, the voices of other people and the calls of the birds. You feel the relaxation, along with the warmth, spreading throughout your body. Close your eyes and spend a few moments enjoying this experience, paying especially close attention to how you feel.

Note: There is no law against anchoring this nice, relaxing, comfortable, stress-free, enjoyable, and useful state, in case you've forgotten.

Step 2:

Now take a few moments to come back to the setting in which you're reading this book. Reorient yourself, and feel comfortable and alert.

Step 3:

This time we'll view the same scene from a different perspective. Imagine you are at the same beach, but this time you are still in the resort hotel across the street from the beach. In fact, you are looking out the window of your room, at least five stories high.

Step 4:

Now, from this vantage point, look down on the beach and imagine *watching yourself* walking onto the beach, five stories below. You can see the water in the distance, and all the sights that were present when you were down on the beach earlier, but from this distant vantage point. You can clearly *see yourself* as you would have looked in the original scene in Step 1, walking on the beach.

Step 5:

Now pay attention to whatever feelings you have at this point. Notice how different they are from the earlier ones you had when you were actually walking along the beach.

Step 6:
Now take a few moments to come back to the room, reorient yourself, and feel comfortable and alert.

I wanted to give you an extra experiment with the visual sub-modality of association & disassociation because it is such a useful one, and people sometimes can use the extra practice. You undoubtedly noticed the different feelings in the two different perspectives. There are several reasons. In the first image, the one of actually being on the beach (associated, looking out through your own eyes) you are able to get back all, or at least some, of the feelings you would normally have during that experience. This is because your brain has catalogued certain feelings that connect to (associate with) specific visual images. That is why, when we remember something vividly, we can get the same feelings back. These images are naturally occurring anchors for those specific feelings.

The second image is quite clearly different both in point of view and the feelings that go with it. Since in this second case you are imagining watching yourself from a distance, your brain has no particular set of feelings to attach to the image. This is because you can't, in reality, see yourself from a distance. This form of artificially constructed visualization is called, again, a *disassociated* image, different from the one you would have if you were really there. So the feelings are disassociated from it as well. It is almost as if you are watching yourself through "someone else's eyes".

In this following experiment, you'll repeat the association and disassociation process you just practiced. This time, though, you'll use this process to assess the viability of the solution you have just come up with, from an objective observer position. Again, read through the instructions before doing the experiment.

EXPERIMENT: TESTING SOLUTIONS – OBJECTIVE OBSERVER

Step 1:

This time imagine, as vividly as possible, what you would look like carrying out the solution you have devised. In other words, run the same movie you ran in the last experiment except, this time, view it from an outside point of view ("fly on the wall"). Pay special attention to the sounds that go with this experience, your own voice and those of other people involved, how the action looks to you, and *how you feel about it* as you watch it from the outside. Remember to run the movie far enough into the future to see the results of your immediate actions.

Step 2:

Ask yourself if everything looks the way it should. Do the other people seem to be responding the way you expected as you watch this movie of yourself? Do you look like you are being effective, and graceful, in your actions? Are you achieving your well formed outcome? Does it look and sound as you hoped it would in your imagination?

Step 3:

If anything looks different from the way you want it to, change it! It's your movie. You can add to it, subtract from it, or change it in any way you see fit.
This may be a good time to use your anchor for your designer state for solving problems again. Treat the image you have seen as new information that you can add into your creative problem solving. Enjoy the process of adjusting your plans, and thank yourself for thinking through these consequences of your actions ahead of time. This is one way we fine tune our solutions.

Step 4:

Jot down some notes about any changes you have made in your solution. Keep these with any other notes you made earlier in this regard.

Step 5:

When you have taken the time to get this movie looking just like you think it ought to, enjoy it for a moment. Ask yourself how you think it will feel to carry out these plans and, as you do, imagine that you can *step back into the movie*. In other words, associate back into the image now, so that you see it as if you are back inside yourself in the movie – back at the beginning.

Step 6:

As you re-run the movie, associated, pay close attention to how you feel. Ask yourself if this is what you expected, and if it is what you want to feel like when you carry out this solution. Do you feel effective and graceful? Is this how you hoped to feel? Is this a more compelling and helpful set of feelings than you had the first time you ran through your solution?

If not, or if this feels *in any way* uncomfortable, immediately step back out of the picture – disassociate. Then re-adjust the image to take care of whatever was bothering you.

Step 7:

Now take a few moments to come back into the room, reorient yourself, and feel comfortable and alert.

Again, it's important to feel comfortable, and even more important to feel motivated to carry through your solution. It is also important to remember that you can repeat the process of disassociating and associating as often as necessary. Be greedy. Get this solution to look, sound, and feel the way you want it. You can repeat this experiment for each and every part of the plan you've developed to solve your problem.

As you might imagine, switching from associated to disassociated images, and back again, can have some other powerful uses. For one thing, as you've undoubtedly discovered on your own, any time you switch to a disassociated image, all of your feelings, and therefore emotions, will diminish considerably, or go away altogether. That is why the man in the seminar had been trained to disassociate by imagining he was up in the air above himself. Any fear or other emotions that would interfere with good judgment can be eliminated in this way. The other result of this shift in perspective is a rational and objective viewpoint on any situation; one that can allow you to make good decisions without undue emotional involvement. This is a useful process to go through from time to time in checking yourself, no matter what the context or situation.

A caution is in order here, however. There are plenty of times when you will want to have emotional input to your judgments and decisions. This is a natural part of decision making most of us refer to as "trusting our gut feelings" or "letting our instincts be our guide". Disassociation is a wonderful tool for determining our present state of affairs, formulating plans of action, and avoiding emotional or physical feelings that get in our way. But usually, once those plans are developed, we want to associate them with how we feel to make sure we don't create other difficulties in the process. In fact, the shift from a disassociated image to an associated one, in other words "stepping back into the picture", can be highly stimulating and motivating.

That experiment of going back and forth from disassociated to associated, adjusting as we go, is called the New Behavior Generator. It was discovered originally as a motivation strategy that many people use, though most people don't realize it while they are using it. It turns out that anyone, by developing a compelling image disassociated, can then jump inside associated again. The part that makes it even more useful, of course, is that it can be used to continually adjust the image until it both *looks right* and *feels right*. Then it can be used for motivation. It can be enhanced even more by using the other sub-modalities along with association and disassociation, like brightening the image, intensifying the colors, turning up the volume of the sounds and so on. By this time, I know that you know how to do that, so feel free to as much as you like.

Now it's time to take yet another point of view in this process; that of each of the others who will be involved. This is a simple process after what we have done so far, and in fact this is very much like the experiment in Chapter 8 called Borrowing Talent. You'll be running the same movie of your solution again, but this time from the point of view of one of the other people. You will want to repeat this for each person you believe to be crucial in your solution. Again read through the instructions first, and then do the experiment.

EXPERIMENT: TESTING SOLUTIONS – THE PERSPECTIVE OF OTHERS

Step 1:
Choose one of the people involved in this situation, who will also be involved in, or affected by, your solution. If you made any notes about their involvement earlier, you may want to look them over again.

Step 2:
Now imagine that you can take this person's place in the movie of your solution. "Step into" the picture and *act as if you are this person*. Do what they do, feel what they feel, think what they think, while the movie runs all the way past the outcome to the results you want. See and hear all of the action through this other person's eyes and ears.

Step 3:
Pay attention to how you *feel* as this person. Is it a good, helpful, motivating feeling? What images do you have in your mind while you act as if you were this other person? What do you hear in your mind, or say to yourself?

Step 4:
Decide how you like it. What would you like to keep? Is there anything you would rather not have, do or experience, as this person – in this situation? What fits, and what doesn't? What would you like to change?

Step 5:
If anything looks different from the way you want it to, again change it. It's still your movie, even though you are in another person's shoes. Make it the way you want it.

Step 6:
Jot down some notes about any changes you have made in this version of your solution. Add them to any other notes you made earlier.

Step 7:
Now take a few moments to come back to the room, reorient yourself, and feel comfortable and alert.

Step 8:
Repeat this entire procedure for each person you have identified as an important part of this situation.

This process of imagining that you are "walking a mile in another man's (or woman's) moccasins" is crucial. If you are someone who sometimes, or often, forgets to consider the needs of others, this is how to do it. It is what considerate people do *naturally*, and what everyone else can learn. It is also a good way of predicting people's reactions to what you propose. This will allow you to do your fine tuning beforehand. Then you can anticipate, and avoid, a lot of the objections you might get otherwise. The process will also enhance your rapport with those you work with by getting you inside their thought processes a bit, just like modeling would do. You may even learn a great deal about yourself, as well.

At this point, you have gone through the solution you came up with from at least three points of view; more if you've repeated the last experiment with different people in mind. These multiple perspectives are the key to wise decision making and problem solving. Wisdom, in fact, can be defined as the ability and willingness to take multiple perspectives. The more you make this a "programmed" part of your behavior, the more you'll be satisfied with your results.

Also, once you have practiced with these multiple viewpoints, it gets much easier. In NLP we have these three viewpoints labeled as first position, second position and third position. Just like in English class, first position is like first person: you (the "I" position). Second position is the same as second person: he or she. Third position is third person: they, or in this case the impartial "fly on the wall" observer. The following diagram should make this even more clear.

Figure 10

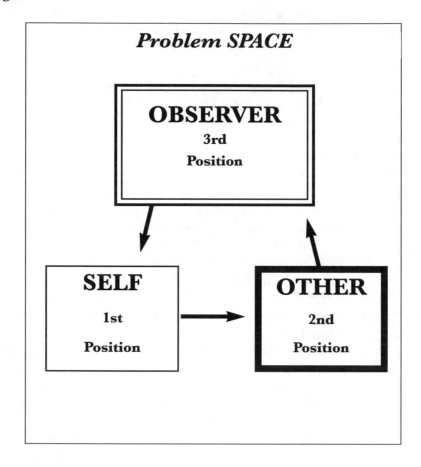

Changing Perceptual Positions

The final experiment is to combine, and continue the process of using these multiple perspectives to fine-tune and enhance your solution(s).

EXPERIMENT: MULTIPLE PERSPECTIVES

Step 1:
Collect all of your notes about changes you've made in the solution and read them again.

Step 2:

Go back to your associated state, *first position*, and run the movie again. Check to make sure that it provides you with the compelling and satisfying feelings you want.

Step 3:

Make any adjustments you need to. Note them down.

Step 4:

Now go to the point of view of one of the other people involved, *second position*, and run the movie again.

Step 5:

Make any adjustments you need to. Note them down.

Step 6:

Repeat second position for each person involved, making necessary adjustments and any notes you may need.

Step 7:

Go to the disassociated viewpoint, *third position*, and run the movie again. Decide whether it looks and sounds the way you would like it to, as an impartial observer.

Step 8:

Make any adjustments, and any notes you need.

Step 9:

Repeat the above sequence, first position, second position and third position, as often as necessary, until you are completely satisfied and compelled to go through with your planned solution from each vantage point.

Notice that I took you through this in a different order this time. We have found that in learning the process of going through all of these different perspectives, for many people it is easiest to go from first to third positions, and then to second. Once you know how to do it, though, you can go in the order of first, second and third to fine tune, as we did here.

SELF WORTH, SELF IMAGE

Most people, at some point in their lives, have wrestled with their own sense of what they are worth; how they "see" themselves. There are several aspects to how we do this inside our minds and, as usual, we have a lot more control over the process than most of us have ever dreamed.

First, we should pay attention to what self image means literally. It is the visual (for most of us) image we have of ourselves in our minds. Disassociated. Literally, how we *see* ourselves. With all we've done with adjusting internal visual images, it should be obvious what we can do with these images. Change them, adjust them, produce the effect we want to have. This goes for what we say about the image, and ourselves, in our minds as well. The combination of the visual image and what we say about it will "drive" our feelings about ourselves. This, of course, will determine how we live and work.

Where do we get the images we have of ourselves? Well, it depends. As we grow up, usually by the time we're teenagers, we have begun to develop a "sense of who we are" by developing these internal images. They're usually determined by what kind of feedback we get from those around us. Family, friends, teachers, and the wider community. We literally go to second and third position to see ourselves through the eyes of others. Later, we get the opportunity to make up our own minds, from our own position, *if we know we have the option.* Some people never learn to make these decisions on their own, or even achieve a balance between what others think, and what they themselves believe.

This balance is probably a great deal of what we mean when we talk about maturity. Most of our teen years are spent learning how much we can run our own lives and how much we have to conform to outside pressures, ideas and rules. If this is a problem you've had, you can apply these exercises on changing the internal images directly to the specific image(s) you have of yourself. Especially changing perceptual positions. People who have really mastered this are those who have good clear images of themselves from each perceptual position, and they *like and respect each one they see* (self-respect). You may surprise yourself with what you can do if you take the time to make your own image. One of the great NLP trainers, Leslie Cameron Bandler taught us a long time ago that if you want to improve your self image, imagine looking at yourself through the eyes of someone who loves you. Try it.

A final note is in order. Many people have fallen into the trap of thinking that their self worth is the same as some random accountant would label it: what you are worth in financial terms, on paper. Everyone is worth a lot more than what the ledger says (regardless of what your banker or loan manager thinks). If you think of yourself as worth, in the area of work, whatever *you are able to produce in real terms,* it looks different than if you think you are worth what you have already produced on paper. And that only relates to your work productivity; only a small part of who you really are. Make sure *you* get to be the one who sets the standards for who you should be. You can model these standards from people you respect, certainly, but you should be the final judge. That is a large part of what it means to really take responsibility for yourself.

Another useful method for fine tuning is to go back to the three processes of creativity we talked about in Chapter 7: The dreamer, the realist and the critic. I have actually incorporated much of this process into the other experiments we have done. We have done the dreamer rather completely, in fact. You can at this stage in the process, however, imagine going through each of the perceptual positions one more time as the critic. Then repeat as the realist. Again make sure that you end up with feelings of satisfaction and are compelled to go forth with your solution (see *Tools for Dreamers*, listed in the Annotated Bibliography, for more).

It might seem like a simple matter to just take action on our plans (or it should be anyway). But we also need to remember to measure our results as we go. The easiest way to do that is to *preset* specific points during the process when the main task is to analyze effectiveness. Many of the standard organizational task analysis or planning charts (such as PERT, CPM, GANNT etc.) are useful for this since they force it into the process. If you are not familiar with these tools, it doesn't really matter. The point is that to be really effective means paying attention to what you are doing, and how it is working.

Now is a good time to decide, if you haven't already, at which points in the process you can measure your effectiveness, and how, exactly, you will do it. This may include actual measurements of some sort, or observations you can rely on. It is important that you build this into the process now, so that you automatically pay attention when you need to. If your outcome was defined in verifiable terms that you can see, hear or feel, going about judging your success should be a straightforward matter. These judgments can be thought of as a function of the critic.

Obviously, careful planning is at least 90% of this process. Just as obviously, there is almost no limit to the amount of planning we could do. When done well, it makes the last 10% smooth, natural, easy, and even fun. But we don't want to get stuck in endless planning, without ever moving forward into action. That is why it is so important to end up with compelling feelings about the actions you have designed for your solution.

RECOMMENDATIONS FOR PRESENTING ORGANIZATIONAL CHANGE

When announcing a change in an organization, for example in a memo, provide motivation, means and opportunity, as we've discussed. The following is a form I've found to be useful for people to follow when giving people the news that things are changing. It respects and prepares for peoples needs and doubts while communicating the most important information those people need to have in making any change. Think about this in meetings and announcements of all kinds and it will help you to focus on the relationship aspects of change as well as the task.

Announcement: (What is being done.)

Description: (What it means, what will be done.)

Who's involved: (People making change & people being affected.)

Reason: (Why it's being done.)

Intended Outcome: (Hoped for result. How the change should achieve it.)

Opportunity for discussion: (Any meetings planned to discuss changes and their effects, and/or whom those involved can talk to about the changes if there are no formal meetings.)

Review date: (When the results will be assessed, measured, discussed.)

Hopefully, this form will give people the rationale behind necessary changes, as well as an understanding of what might be accomplished. In other words, "There is a problem, here is a solution, this is when we will make sure it worked." It will also give them a better understanding of how the organization is run, the challenges and difficulties, and how to think through solving problems. It should also help make them feel a part of what happens and affects them.

Finally, this form may be useful in all memos, though it can be modified as you see fit. Remember, though, a memo never replaces direct communication, it only announces things to be done and discussed later.

If you do not have these compelling feelings at this point, you might look back to your well formed outcome. Does it still seem to be what you want? Let's take another look at the conditions for a well formed outcome to be sure. The first two conditions for determining a well-formed outcome are usually well ingrained in whatever you have done up to this point. They are:

1.   The outcome is **stated in positive** terms.
2.   The outcome is **applied to yourself.**

In fact I can't imagine how you could have gotten this far without meeting these conditions all along the way. Primarily, at this point, we are interested in the last three conditions of your outcome. Once you have carried out your plan, it is a good idea to double check and make sure that you have indeed met these.

3.   The outcome is **readily verifiable in sensory terms**.
4.   The outcome is **placed in the proper context**.
5.   The outcome **maintains the positive by-products of previous situations and behavior**.

These conditions should have been thoroughly insured by this time in the process, if you went through all of the experiments thoroughly. If not it's probably quite obvious what needs to be done.

When you are fully satisfied, and compelled to go forward and carry out your plan, anchor this state. Then you can use this anchor to compel you through to your solution any time you find yourself getting bogged down.

The Aftermath

After you carry out your plan, you may want to take a look back at the process in hindsight. That way you can streamline it for future use. You may have found that some things you did automatically, which allowed you to skip some of the steps. By the same token, you may find that there are other steps you would do well to practice and make an ongoing part of your behavior. You may also want to answer these following questions, as you did earlier, and find out if you get pretty much the same kinds of answers.

1. Have you really achieved what you set out to do? Can you see and hear the results you wanted; are they readily verifiable to you now?
2. Have you limited the effects of what you've accomplished so that your solution properly changes the situation(s) you intended, without spilling over into unwanted territory? Did you do what you intended in the right time and place?
3. Have you managed to preserve whatever by-products are necessary and worthwhile having, now that you have made these changes (have you avoided "throwing out the baby with the bath water")?
4. Have you maintained the important relationships you had during the process?

Provided you can answer all those questions, now, with satisfaction, you can be pretty sure that you have accomplished a worthwhile goal by solving this problem. In addition, it could be wise to look back over your long-term outcomes, personal beliefs and values to insure that you have kept all of these aligned while making these changes. If you can say that you have: Congratulations, you've done it!

Part II

Using States Of Consciousness

Underview

Going through these processes systematically is a very unusual approach for most people. I am striving to make this kind of thinking, and the technical procedures that go along with it, available to the general public in as many ways as possible. Solving problems in the business community is only one of these. I trust your success will provide the encouragement you need to pursue this brand of thinking, planning and problem solving.

You should now know how to control your state of mind better than ever before. This, and the order of events we went through, forms the heart, and the guts, of this problem solving model. Doing the experiments carefully and thoroughly can form the basis for a great deal of planning and management strategy development for you–from now on. It is also possible to implement these methods on the group, team or even organizational level. You can use the model to develop strategies for this implementation itself.

I'm sure that it is now obvious that the experiments I have guided you through were meant to do a great deal more than just solve one problem. The technology in this second half of the book is one which can change your life in an untold number of ways. I hope you will continue to explore. Also, it should be obvious that this kind of problem solving need not be limited to the business arena. In fact, much of it can be applied beyond problem solving as well. You have only to begin.

Appendix

APPENDIX

This appendix section of the book is meant to be a resource guide for you once you have gone through Part I and Part II and know how to use the tools. The major resources are listed here so that you can quickly remind yourself of the procedures, rules, lists and guidelines for each process in this problem solving model. Each one includes a reminder of the specific chapter it is covered in, so that you can easily refer back to the proper section for more detail and explanation. Here is what is contained in this appendix:

Contents

APPENDIX I

Resources from Part I

Presuppositions of NLP (From Chapter 1)

Conditions for Well-Formed Outcomes (From Chapter 2)

Meta-Program Questions (From Chapter 3)

The Seven C's (From Chapter 4)

Neuro-Logical Levels (From Chapter 4)

The Problem Types (From Chapter 5)

PRESUPPOSITIONS OF NLP

This is the list of important basic assumptions underlying everything I have presented to you in this book. See Chapter 1 for a fuller explanation.

Presupposition #1:
The map *is not* the territory

Presupposition #2:
All behavior has some "positive" intention. People make the best choices they perceive are available to them.

Presupposition #3:
The meaning of any communication is the response it elicits, regardless of the communicator's intent.

Presupposition #4:
The mind/body relationship is cybernetic; a change in one part of the system will affect other parts.

Presupposition #5:
There are no mistakes, only outcomes. There are no failures, only feedback.

Presupposition #6:
Everyone has all of the internal resources they really need – which doesn't mean they couldn't use a little help finding them.

Presupposition #7:
All the information you need can be obtained through clear and open sensory channels.

Presupposition #8:
An effective person (in business and life) needs three characteristics:
    1. Flexibility of behavior to get results.
    2. The sensory acuity to notice the results.
    3. The good judgement to know whether the results are worth getting.

Presupposition #8 Corollary 1:

Resistance is a sign that:

Either

Rapport has not been effectively established or maintained.

Or

Objections have not been properly considered and addressed.

Presupposition #8 Corollary 2:

There is no such thing as a dangerous or unethical process or technique, only dangerous and unethical users (people). It is up to us to know the difference and act accordingly.

Presupposition #9:

If it is possible in the world, it is possible for anyone. It is only a question of how.

CONDITIONS FOR WELL-FORMED OUTCOMES

Here is a reminder of the necessary conditions for developing an outcome that is well-formed, i.e. specific, achievable and measurable. See Chapter 2 For a more detailed explanation.

1. The outcome is **stated in positive terms**.
   The outcome must be stated in terms of what you *want*–not what you *don't want*. Watch out for words indicating negation such as don't, won't, shouldn't, can't, stop, etc. Remember negation ("no") does not exist in experience, it only exists in language; just a shorthand to make communication quicker, not more effective.

2. The outcome is **applied to yourself**.
   You must focus on what you can do, and be responsible for, not others. Even if the outcome involves others, you can only be sure of how you will behave, and, from that, only predict how those actions may effect what others do or think.

3. The outcome is **readily verifiable in sensory terms**.
   Make sure you can see, hear, or feel the results of your actions, and the outcome itself. An outcome or goal needs to be specific. Nebulous outcomes seldom lead to decisive, well directed action.

4. The outcome is **placed in the proper context**.
   Make sure you change or produce an outcome, or even any specific behavior, only when and where it will have the desired effect(s), and not in inappropriate situations. A well-formed outcome is specific in form (what), as above, and also in context (where, when and with who).

5. The outcome **maintains the positive by-products of previous situations and behavior**.

Sometimes even problem behavior or situations are doing some good. It is important not to throw out that good, while trying to improve the situation and solve problems. Also, it is wise to check through all the possible ramifications of achieving the outcome (or solving the problem), and the behavior leading to it. This will insure that new and unforeseen problems, or unfortunate consequences, aren't created as well.

META-PROGRAM QUESTIONS

These questions are repeated here for you to use whenever you think you need to plan for the involvement, support or help of another person. See Chapter 3 for a fuller explanation.

Convincers

1. What convinces this person of the value of something? Do they rely on what is in front of them, here and now, or do they need to see results over a **TIME PERIOD**? How long a time period would be necessary to convince this person, or group of people, of the worth of your ideas?

2. Are they more likely to pay attention to **PAST** experiences, **PRESENT** contacts and presentations, or the promise of **FUTURE** benefits, services or guarantees?

3. Would they need to see a certain **NUMBER** of successes, **EXAMPLES** of positive experiences, to make a judgment, perhaps independent of how much time it takes?

4. In making their judgments, would they need to **SEE** results, or **READ** reports of effectiveness? Would they need to **HEAR** from other people who have had experience with you or what you propose? Would they need their own **EXPERIENCE**, say a trial run or sample of some sort? Do they have to "**FEEL** it's right".

5. How about the five great questions: Who, What, Where, When, or How–to convince this person of what you propose?

Motivators

1. Is the person you are dealing with more likely to be **PROACTIVE** or **REACTIVE**? In other words will this person be likely, or even able, to act on his or her own initiative? Is he or she more likely to wait for something to happen, and then respond (*act*, or *reac*

2. The most important question may be, can this person act at all, or does he or she have to wait for *someone else* to make a decision? Depending on the answer to that question, are you certain, right now, that you are dealing with the right person?

3. Assuming that this is the right person, or one of the right people, do they rely heavily on **EXTERNAL** information, that which comes from others to make decisions, or on what they feel and think based on their own **INTERNAL** processes (gut reactions, clearly thought out procedures, etc.)? How can you use this information to help both of you achieve your goals?

4. Does this person tend to operate **TOWARD** pleasure, success and possibility, or **AWAY FROM** pain, and perceived problems? In other words, does he or she respond to fear and punishment (sticks) or pleasure and rewards (carrots)?

5. If you don't know, can you gracefully include both as possibilities in your communication with them? Can you show the negative consequences of not taking your advice or suggestions, while at the same time showing the advantages of following your lead?

6. Will this person respond to your presentation because of the **POSSIBILITIES** involved, or because they perceive they have no other choice, i.e. out of **NECESSITY**?

7. Will this person likely respond to how your products, services, ideas or proposals **MATCH** something he or she is already familiar with? Or, on the other hand, do you need to show how what you offer is a **MISMATCH** for what is expected such as a unique feature of some sort? In other words, does this person look for things that are the **SAME** as something they are already familiar with, or things that are **DIFFERENT**, when making a decision? If you don't know, can you include features of both sameness and difference in what you present?

Thinking Style

1. It is possible to focus one's attention more to small details, or to more general, abstract ideas. Which should you concentrate on? Should you start with **GENERAL** ideas and move toward more **SPECIFIC** ones in your dealings with this person? Perhaps the other way around? Does this person have, or need, to "see the big picture" to act on something, or would they rather a series of small details?

2. Can you list, in **ORDER OF PRIORITY**, the things relevant to your proposal that you think are most important to this person or group of people? How can you organize your thinking, or the content of your presentation, that will respect, appreciate, and, most of all, respond directly to their priorities?

3. Finally, are there some **RULES** that this person chooses, or is forced to follow, in responding to you? How can you make it easy for them to follow these rules while responding favorably to you in the process?

THE SEVEN C'S

The Seven C's model covers the many ways we can sabotage ourselves and ruin our conviction and drive toward our outcomes. But, for each problem there is a cure. See Chapter 4 for a more thorough explanation.

THE SEVEN C's

Conundrums		Cures
Confusion	———>	Clarity
Content	———>	Consistency
Conflict	———>	Consensus
Catastrophe	———>	Conviction
Conviction	———>	Congruency
Context	———>	Creativity
Comparison	———>	Communication

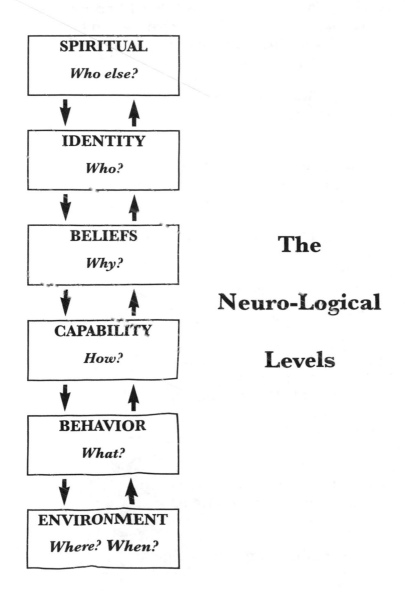

SPIRITUAL
Who else?

IDENTITY
Who?

BELIEFS
Why?

CAPABILITY
How?

BEHAVIOR
What?

ENVIRONMENT
Where? When?

The

Neuro-Logical

Levels

THE PROBLEM TYPES

This somewhat arbitrary list is what I find most useful in identifying a particular problem so that we can best design an approach to developing solutions. See Chapter 5 for a much more thorough explanation.

1. Personal (individual) problems
    a) Creativity/Innovation
    b) Motivation
    c) Focus
    d) Planning, productivity & limitations
    e) Tools, materials, support, time/space
    f) Neuro-logical levels

2. Interpersonal/Communication problems
    a) Vision
    b) Intention
    c) Clarity, Understanding
    d) Rapport
    e) Objections

3. Training problems
    a) Training effectiveness
    b) Knowledge, Skills & Procedures
    c) Systemic effects
    d) Neuro-logical level effects

4. Systemic problems
    a) Design flaws & communication
    b) Timing & System reverberation

5. Environmental/Situational problems

APPENDIX II

Resources from Part II

Sub-Modalities (From Chapter 6)

List of Universally Valuable States (From Chapter 7)

State Design Method & Work Sheet (From Chapter 8)

Guidelines for Effective Anchoring (From Chapter 9)

SUB-MODALITIES

(See Chapter 6 for complete descriptions of each of these sub-modality distinctions and their uses.)

VISUAL

Brightness	Focus
Distance	Slide
Size	Motion Picture
Shape	Movement/Speed
Location	Associated
Direction	Disassociated
Contrast	Depth 3D/Flat
Clarity	Frame/No Frame
Color	Other?

AUDITORY

Sounds	Timbre
Words	Internal
Location	External
Pitch	Direction
Tone	Tempo
Voice (Who?)	Volume
Distance	Duration
Rhythm	Other?

KINESTHETIC

Internal	Proprioceptive
External	Shape
Location	Temperature
Weight	Movement
Duration	Intensity
Size	Moisture
Pressure	Texture
Frequency	Rhythm
Tactile	Balance
Emotion?	Other?

OLFACTORY

Sweet
Sour
Salty
Bitter
Specific taste

GUSTATORY

Pungent
Intensity
Location
Aromatic
Specific smell

LIST OF UNIVERSALLY VALUABLE STATES

While there is probably no perfect list of states you could develop that would be useful, these are the ones I've identified as most universally helpful in problem solving. Each is covered in Chapter 7 in some detail, so you might want to look back over the descriptions. I can't emphasize enough how helpful it can be to have the ability, and therefore the choice, to use these states and the resources that go along with them, at will.

Openness to Change
Learning
Taking Other Viewpoints: Perspective
Creativity
Focus
Planning, Setting Goals & Outcomes
Handling Constraints or Adversity
Breaking Habits
Taking Action, Motivation
Willingness to Take Risks
Feeling Safe & Secure
Decision Making
Clarity and Understanding
Developing Effective Relationships
Gaining & Maintaining Rapport
Being Healthy
Finishing

STATE DESIGN METHOD & WORK SHEET

Here are the steps, repeated for you, for getting into a particular state and filling out the DESIGNER STATE WORK SHEET. You may want to make extra copies of the work sheets to have on hand. Since you have gone through this and similar exercises so many times, it should seem second nature by now, but see Chapter 8 for further explanation if you need to, or to remind yourself of the times you have already done this.

Step 1:

Remember the last time you had this particular state and go back into it now. Imagine you are back in the time and place you had this powerful and useful state.

Jot down a note on the copy of the Designer State Work Sheet on the line that says Descriptive Label. This can be a note about the original memory or anything else to remind you of exactly which state this is. It could even be a name, if you wish to give this state one. This is just to remind you about the nature of the experience when you use this in the future.

Then fill in a sentence or two on the lines labeled Description of Content. These can be notes about the actual images you see and hear, as well as any comments about the feelings you have as you look and listen to these images in your mind.

Step 2:

Experience this state for a moment and pay close attention to all of the important feelings you have while you're in this state.

While you are having these feelings, fill out the KINES-THETIC portion of the work sheet by making any notes about the sub-modalities you think are important. The more thorough a job you do on this, the more it will help you in the future.

Step 3:

Next carefully examine whatever internal visual image you have as you re-experience this special state. Take a moment to fill out the VISUAL portion of the sheet now, just as you did on the kinesthetic section. Examine the picture in your mind thoroughly enough to make notes on all of the sub modalities you can.

Step 4:

Now, pay close attention to the sounds you have in your mind. This could be your own voice as you talk to yourself about how excited you are. It could be someone else's voice that you imagined hearing during the original experience. It could be any other type of sound, as well, from music to bells to fireworks. The brain is a creative organ. When you can clearly hear all that is going on in your mind, fill out the AUDITORY portion of the sheet.

Step 5:

If you are aware of any outstanding smells or tastes as you experience this state, make notes about those now as well.

What you'll have now is a complete description of the content and the sub-modalities of this state. In fact, the work sheet itself could become an anchor for you. Also, you could certainly enhance the intensity of the feelings in this state by adjusting the sub-modalities as you did earlier.

DESIGNER STATE WORK SHEET

Descriptive Label_____

Description of Content_____

_____

VISUAL

Brightness	_____	Focus	_____
Distance	_____	Slide	_____
Size	_____	Motion Picture	_____
Shape	_____	Movement/Speed	_____
Location	_____	Associated	_____
Direction	_____	Disassociated	_____
Contrast	_____	Depth 3D/Flat	_____
Clarity	_____	Frame/No Frame	_____
Color	_____	Other?	_____

AUDITORY

Sounds	_____	Timbre	_____
Words	_____	Internal	_____
Location	_____	External	_____
Pitch	_____	Direction	_____
Tone	_____	Tempo	_____
Voice (Who?)	_____	Volume	_____
Distance	_____	Duration	_____
Rhythm	_____	Other?	_____

KINESTHETIC

Internal	_____	Proprioceptive	_____
External	_____	Shape	_____
Location	_____	Temperature	_____
Weight	_____	Movement	_____
Duration	_____	Intensity	_____
Size	_____	Moisture	_____
Pressure	_____	Texture	_____
Frequency	_____	Rhythm	_____
Tactile	_____	Balance	_____
Emotion?	_____	Other?	_____

OLFACTORY/GUSTATORY

Sweet	_____	Pungent	_____
Sour	_____	Intensity	_____
Salty	_____	Location	_____
Bitter	_____	Aromatic	_____
Specific taste	_____	Specific smell	_____

Description of Anchor_____

_____

GUIDELINES FOR EFFECTIVE ANCHORING

These are the guidelines I gave you in Chapter 9, as a quick reminder.

1. Make each anchor *distinct* from anything else you normally do or it will be contaminated by ("collapsed with") all the other states you go into when you fire the anchor. In other words, if you hold your thumb and forefinger together, as a habit, on a regular basis, use something else for the anchor you want. Otherwise, you'll be firing it all the time and it will slowly "dilute" itself to nothing.

2. Make sure you are *really in the state* you want anchored, not just thinking about what it should be like. You will anchor whatever state you are in when you set up the anchor–for better or worse–the anchor doesn't care which.

3. Anchors should be *tested* for effectiveness when they are set. Make sure you anchored what you want to have, in yourself (or in others) by first breaking the state, then firing the anchor to insure that the resource state returns. The reason it is important to break the state first is that, if you are already in it, you won't know if the anchor really produces it at will.

4. It may take several tries to get the anchor to work. This is especially true when you are first learning since you may have to practice duplicating placement and timing. Be patient, and give yourself a reasonable number of attempts. Also, if you have trouble with one kind of anchor (touch, words, etc.) choose another.

5. Anchors can be "stacked" meaning they combine in strength and quality, by setting the same anchor for several *similar* useful states. (Anchors can also be "collapsed" on each other, effectively canceling each other out; a method for getting rid of unwanted anchors (this is beyond this book so check the bibliography for more information.)

6. Anchors can work in any representational system (sensory modality). Practice using touch, hand and facial gestures, and voice tones and inflections. Anchors are all around us, and inside of our thinking processes. They cannot be avoided but they can be controlled. Remember: ANCHORS WORK! So use them wisely.

7. The more internal awareness and sensory acuity you have, the easier it will be to insure success. You'll know if you are in the desired state or not. And the more external awareness and sensory acuity the better in working with others (also beyond the scope of this book).

APPENDIX III:

The NeuroLink

Most people have at least heard of biofeedback, the process of training people to control certain responses like tension, headaches, high blood pressure and the like. It is available in most hospitals and is a fairly simple set of procedures. The patient is hooked up to devices which measure physiological variables like blood pressure, muscle tension, galvanic skin response (gsr, the electrical conductivity, and therefore moisture level, on the surface of the skin), heart rate, temperature and so on. As the devices register their readings, the patient can watch gauges or lights, listen to tones, or get some other *feedback* about what is going on in his or her body.   The devices give instant results the patient can respond to. Then he or she can "learn" to control these physiological responses.

Of course, what the patient actually learns in this process is to control his or her state, in much the same way I've described in this book.

The NeuroLink is a set of hardware devices and software that can be hooked up to your own personal computer. It provides these biofeedback hookups so that you can learn to control your states, while your computer tells you, very precisely, how well you're doing. This system was designed by Robert Dilts and is based on the NLP principles you've been reading about and using throughout this book.

The hardware is very simple. Small leads are strapped to your right hand, left hand or both. These measure galvanic skin response, heart rate and/or skin temperature, depending on which configuration you want. In fact, you can hook up to 32 people up at one time! Your computer takes the information and can do a variety of things with it to help you learn to control your states. It will also store all of these states for later reference – like an electronic version of our DESIGNER STATE WORK SHEETS.

There are a number of user-friendly software packages available to run with the NeuroLink. The one that most resembles what we have done in this book is called the State

Enhancement Coach (SEC). The SEC will gather physiological information from the leads, gsr, heart rate and temperature. It will also ask you questions about posture and physiological positioning, and information about your internal images, sounds and feelings. From this it will measure a reference state that you can name, just as you did on the work sheets during your experiments in this book. You can create these states for anything we covered, as well as any other states you would like.

The software uses sophisticated artificial intelligence procedures to record and compare any of your states. The computer actually "learns" to distinguish between states and determine specific physiological patterns for each one. It can then tell you, very precisely, how close you are to any state you have designed. It can even give you very detailed reports which describe both the physiological components, and the internal processing components (images, sounds, feelings and sub-modalities).

SEC will actually coach you to help you learn to quickly get into your best states at will. It can coach you in one of five different ways.

1. ***Biofeedback***. The computer can give you direct measures of specific physiological responses you are giving at any moment in time. It does this by traditional biofeedback methods, like you might see in a hospital biofeedback lab.

2. ***Cognitive***. It can also remind you of certain key elements in your thinking to guide you closer into your state. This is like looking at your DESIGNER STATE WORK SHEET to remember an image, or set of sub-modalities, but the computer does it automatically.

3. ***Icarus***. The ancient Greek myth of Icarus provides an actual *biofeedback game* you can play, while you learn to control your state. You'll see a picture of mountains, the ocean below, and the Sun above. Icarus needs to fly from one mountain top to another (or to a specific target spot), without falling into the water or flying too close to the Sun (if he gets too close his wings will melt and he'll fall into the water). Specific states can be programmed by the computer to give you targets to aim Icarus to on the screen. Each target is determined by

a particular state you desire. You actually control the flight of Icarus by controlling your state. Lots more fun than playing a computer game with a joystick!

4. ***Unite the Planet***. You'll see four pieces of the planet Earth, one in each of the four corners of the computer screen. Again, controlling your state controls the motion of each one. If you can bring them all together, you've hit your target state. As you intensify, or enhance your state, the planet begins to spin.

5. ***Body Systems***. This method gives you elaborate graphical information on a wide variety of different physiological responses you are exhibiting. A very interesting and educational way to learn about yourself, your physiology and your states.

The main advantage of the NeuroLink is its infinite patience. You can take all the time you need to learn to control your states. It can store hundreds of them, depending on how much room you have in your computer. It is amazingly accurate and a lot of fun as well.

You could easily store each problem solving state you designed while going through the book, plus many more as you continue to do the experiments whenever you need to. The SEC will permanently record all the data for you so that you can solve problems easily and effectively from now on.

This is one of the most advanced uses for computers today. Actually helping us be better people is what they are all about. Finally, we have hardware and software that can actually do it.

For more information, or to order NeuroLink:

NeuroLink
343 Soquel Ave., #334
Santa Cruz, Ca. 95062
Phone: (408) 438-5679
Fax: (408) 438-5649

APPENDIX IV

A LOOK AT NLP'S UNDERSIDE

Modeling

Since NLP is based on human modeling, a note on modeling (literally building models) is in order. It actually means finding and describing the important elements and processes that people go through to do something, as I said. The process starts with finding and studying a *human model*. This is a person, who does something in a particular, usually highly skillful, way. It's a great method for learning about people and how they do things. For example, if you want to know how to serve a tennis ball, you'd first find someone who does it extremely well. There are lots of them. Then ask him or her lots of questions about what they do, why they do it, what works and doesn't work, and so on. At the same time, observing this person in action will often lead to new and better questions to ask in the process. Adding NLP technology makes it possible to discover much of what this human model does that he or she is not even aware of.

When this is done properly, taking the time, using the technology, and applying a good bit of logic, a new *working model* is the result. This new model is actually a set of instructions. If it's good, it can be used by anyone who wants to duplicate the skills and abilities of the human model who was the original subject. In other words, we could all serve a tennis ball like the pro we modeled. It would take effort and practice certainly (like most worthwhile activities) but much less than if we learned in more traditional ways.

This is not the only kind of modeling though. It is also possible to build a *model of a process* itself. One that can be used in different situations. For example, several years ago I participated in a project to discover and describe the processes of *writing* comfortably, easily (within reason) and well. This involved more than just asking a number of people who write to describe their opinions, habits, strategies, and beliefs. It was also necessary to decide what the actual tasks of producing good written material are. Then, what must happen inside someone's mind while they are performing each of these separate writing tasks. Interviewing writers showed, beyond a doubt, that what they *think* and *say* they do is *not* what they actually do. So part of the project involved aligning people's statements and ideas with their actual, sometimes very different, behavior.

This is something that occurs in all of us. In fact it occurs just about any time someone tries to teach someone else to do something. Think about it for a moment. Have you ever taught someone to do something? Were you aware, when you started, of all the things you do to be effective at it? Did you find the person you were teaching asked you reasonable questions you simply could not answer–even though you could *do* what you were teaching?

It turns out that people are very rarely aware of very much of what they actually do, especially in their thinking processes. Their explanations give only a part of the total picture. The modeler, using logic, and testing his or her findings along the way, fills in the rest; or outright discovers differences between what people say they do and what they actually do. In that case the wise modeler throws out what they say, and believes what they do.

Redundancy

There are a couple of principles from designing computer programs that seem applicable here. One is redundancy. If you cover all the bases, and certain potentially troublesome ones *more than is necessary*, you build in safeguards. This is wise. I've built in some safeguards into the Solution States process. Not that there is really any danger in them; just extra measures to insure that you use all the processes without skipping any crucial steps. So, at times, you may find some of the procedures to be repetitive or even tedious. When you discover this, be thankful that you have noticed it. It means that you've followed instructions well and already accomplished something adequately the first time. It can't hurt to do it again.

Repetition and redundancy are good ways to be thorough. Another way is to be recursive, another common pattern in computer programming. What it means is that when you get to a certain point, you might have the opportunity to go back through a section of the process again. This time though, instead of just repeating something, you usually do it in a new or different way. For our purposes, this "looping back" through a segment of the process allows you to take different viewpoints into account, approach solutions in various ways, or make refinements that will insure success and greater efficiency. Some things in life are never really complete or perfect.

Let's look back to our example of writing. Often writing is "finished" when it is *time* to be, or when no further improvements can be justified. That seldom means it's perfect. It usually just means it's as close as realistically possible, within some limitations. Music is the same. There is probably no such thing as the "perfect" performance. Sooner or later someone has to make the decision that rehearsing just won't help much more; or perhaps that the compact disc needs to be produced while the musicians are still young enough to go on tour to sell it. Rehearsing music is a useful kind of recursion, especially if something is added in each practice run. This is true for the process of editing writing until it is as good as it can get. The same principle can be applied to developing workable solutions to problems.

Theory?

Often people ask about the theory behind some new explanation, or description of anything they hear or read about. That's fine so long as the person asking isn't just looking for a way to have a useless argument, or get away without trying something new. Too often people will get into long detailed accounts of what is wrong with the theory behind some new procedure, without ever trying to find out if it works. That's silly. The proverbial bottom line should be effectiveness, not theoretical perfection. But people are often lazy. Some would rather find a reason to avoid doing something new, even in the face of some problem they can't solve, than risk new effort at a solution. I trust, if you have picked up this book, that you take yourself more seriously than that.

One of the real issues for most people is fear of the unknown. It is much easier, and seems safer, to do what's familiar. In fact, this "drive" to stay with the familiar is the strongest one that people have. Stronger even than the will to survive; otherwise why would so many people continue to do self-destructive things rather than change? It does little good to tell someone repeatedly that they are hurting themselves, or others, it they are too afraid of changing to stop. A better plan is to give them something that makes sense to them, appears as safe as possible, is within their immediate abilities, and will actually work.

So, now to the question of our basic theory in NLP. We don't really have one. NLP is not based on theory. It is a set of models. There is a big difference. A model doesn't have to be "true" or "correct" or even perfectly formed. It only has to be useful. If it isn't, it can be discarded in any situation where it fails. A theory, on the other hand, especially in the area of human behavior, can't be discarded easily. Generally when some *behavioral* theory doesn't hold up to scrutiny, or doesn't match up well with experience, the person defending the theory will simply try to re-explain it, argue with the findings, or call the challenger names. When a model doesn't work, we shrug our shoulders and try something else. In NLP, for me, and in this book, the bottom line is results. Not reasons. If at any time the Solution States process doesn't work for you, after diligent effort and attention to instruction, I apologize. I also suggest you go try something else.

Annotated Bibliography of Introductory NLP Books

Note: At the time of publication, there are over 100 books available on NLP. Trying to pick one up, at random, is risky. Follow the advice here, or ask someone, an NLP Practitioner (or Trainer, preferably) familiar with the literature, before starting out. As you might imagine, with so many titles, some are great, some are awful, many are very confusing without some background, workshops or training. This list is intended to introduce some good starting points only. It isn't intended to be complete in any way. Most people find it easiest, from this list, to begin with *Meta-Cation, Vol. I, Beyond Selling*, or for a more self-help oriented book, *Heart of the Mind*.

Andreas, Steve & Connirae: *Heart of the Mind*. Moab, Utah, Real People Press, 1989.
A nice self-help oriented introduction to NLP. Each chapter is essentially a technique that you can do yourself to make a change in something you would like to be different. Everything from phobias to decision making is covered in discussion, demonstration and instruction.

Bagley, Dan S. III and Edward J. Reese: *Beyond Selling* Cupertino, Ca., Meta Publications, 1987.
Very good, easy to read, introduction to NLP in sales. Includes an excellent section on establishing, maintaining and using rapport with customers.

Bandler, Richard: *Using your Brain, for a Change* Moab, Utah, Real People Press, 1987.
Basic self-help with NLP, taken from transcripts of workshops with Richard Bandler, one of the co-developers of NLP. Covers sub-modalities in a wide variety of ways and uses. Easy to follow and also very clever and funny in spots.

Bandler, Richard and John Grinder: *Frogs into Princes* Moab, Utah, Real People Press, 1979.

> The "classic" introduction to NLP, also taken from transcripts of early workshops with Bandler and Grinder. Not as easy to follow for most people. Covers anchoring, changing past experiences and a very useful process called reframing. Easier to follow after introductory seminars in NLP for most business people and then only if helping others is a goal.

Dilts, Robert: *Applications of NLP.* Cupertino, Ca., Meta Publications, 1983.

> An introduction to many uses of the basics of NLP technology by one of the early masters. Actually written as a series of articles, all of which are fairly easy reading. Includes chapters on business communication, sales, negotiation and more.

Dilts, Robert: *Strategies of Genius, Vols. I, II & III* Cupertino, Ca., Meta Publications, 1994, 1995.

> A fascinating series of books identifying and explaining the specific thinking strategies of a number of geniuses throughout history including Albert Einstein, Sigmund Freud, Aristotle, Nicola Tesla and more. Dilts has been doing research in this area for many years and has the ability to take these thinking strategies and put them into everyday terms and use.

Dilts, Robert: *Visionary Leadership Skills.* Cupertino, Ca., Meta Publications, 1996.

> A terrific book on leadership, what it means, how to develop and use it. Filled with exercises and strategies every business (and any other kind of) leader can learn from and use.

Dilts, Robert B., Todd Epstein and Robert W. Dilts: *Tools for Dreamers: Strategies for Creativity and the Structure of Innovation.*

> This is a fascinating look at creativity. Includes a much more thorough description of the Dreamer, Realist and Critic model and how to use it. Also interviews with several very creative geniuses, analyzed to elicit their strategies so that the reader can try them out.

Dilts, Robert B. & Gino Bonissone: *Skills for the Future: Managing Creativity and Innovation.* Cupertino, Ca., Meta Publications, 1993.
A companion book to Tools For Dreamers, this book is filled with charts and guides to help you with your creativity, and managing it with others and in groups. It is based on years of research in one of the largest companies in the world: Fiat.

Jacobson, Sid: *Meta-Cation: Prescriptions For Some Ailing Educational Processes.* Cupertino, Ca., Meta Publications, 1983. *Meta-Cation, Vol. II: New Improved Formulas For Thinking About Thinking.* Cupertino, Ca., Meta Publications, 1986.
Meta-Cation, Vol. III: Powerful Applications For Strong Relief. Cupertino, Ca., Meta Publications, 1986.
Good, easy to read, introduction to NLP. Written for teachers and parents, but understandable to everyone. Contains a number of exercises, including anchoring, collapsing anchors to get rid of unwanted states, and using basic NLP technology to help others. Volume II is a more advanced look at the NLP model, with lots of examples. More philosophical about both NLP and education in America, but still highly readable. Exercises geared to the procedures described in Vol. III. The most advanced and best written of this series. They must be read in order, however, to make any sense.

Jacobson, Sid: *Neuro-Linguistic Programming.* INFO-LINE, American Society For Training & Development, April, 1994.
An introduction to the uses of NLP in business designed for training and human resource professionals.

About the Author

Sid Jacobson has been working in NLP since 1978, and was one of the early Trainers Certified by the Society of NLP. Though beginning as a psychotherapist, he has worked broadly in NLP, as a researcher, trainer, and consultant to professionals, hospitals, schools, clinics, businesses, public and private organizations, and both amateur and private athletes. He holds a Ph.D. in Clinical Psychology and is considered to be an expert in the application of NLP to education and training, having written the three volume set titled Meta-Cation - a classic series in the application of NLP to education - in addition to a number of books, papers and articles on NLP. He founded and directs the South Central Institute of NLP in New Orleans. Sid currently consults and trains throughout the U.S., in South America, Canada, Great Britain and Asia. He lives in New Orleans with his wife Cindi Lanza.

If you wish to contact Sid Jacobson, write to:

Sid Jacobson, Ph.D.
Director
South Central Institute of NLP
P.O. Box 1213, Mandeville, Louisiana 70470
USA
email: sidjacob@pipeline.com